Praise for *The Joy Filled Soul*

Reading *The Joy Filled Soul* feels like you have a friend and mentor sitting next to you in the struggles of life. Janine provides helpful insights born out of her own journey of pursuing God's heart even when it's not easy. By her example you feel uplifted and supported to take God at His Word, to wrestle with unpleasant emotions, and to continue to trust that He is in control. Life outside of Eden is very unpredictable, which often steals our natural sense of happiness. *The Joy Filled Soul* gives us an anchor for stability and fresh wisdom for how to tap into the supernatural resources available to God's people who find themselves in turbulent times.

—Dr. CHRISTY HILL, Director of Ignite 31:26 Ministries and Professor of Spiritual Formation and Women's Ministries at Grace Theological Seminary

The Joy Filled Soul is exactly what we need in these times of change and uncertainty. Through vulnerability, Janine unpacks God's unconditional gift of joy in a relatable way. As I was reading, I felt as though we were sitting across the table from one another sharing coffee and Jesus. Janine's desire for every woman to be filled with God's joy jumps off the pages and I finished reading feeling both encouraged and motivated. This is a book that will challenge our perceptions of joy in a loving way with the purpose of leading us to a deeper understanding of God's gift to us.

—KAITLYN AMADOR, Coordinator for MOPS Off the Clock at Crossline Church

Life's challenges can cast dark shadows on our souls, but despair doesn't have to get the final word. Join Janine Lansing on her journey to joy and find some helpful insights for your own spiritual expedition.

—Melissa Spoelstra, Bible teacher, women's conference speaker, author of seven Bible studies, and contributor to Proverbs 31 Ministries First 5 App

From the first lines of the introduction, Janine's wise words about joy captured my heart. I have been on a journey to understand and know joy deep in my soul and this book is just what I needed. Janine's down to earth, honest approach to calling readers into a joy filled life is something you won't want to miss. This book brought me to the throne of Jesus and reminded me that I already have access to soul deep joy through Him.

—Dr. Nicole Miller, Director of Girls' Ministry for Sisters Mentoring with a Mission, a ministry of Women of Grace USA

Genuine, relational, and inspiring, *The Joy Filled Soul* is a message that will powerfully impact the way you live and experience life. Janine intimately invites you to step out in faith and honestly search the depths of your soul to find the answers to the longings and aches of your heart and gives practical steps to mend the broken and bruised places. Writing from a place of vulnerability about her own struggles with finding and keeping joy, Janine talks to you like a dear friend who deeply desires you to experience the joy she now has. Her enthusiasm is contagious and motivated by a deep love for our Creator. You won't be disappointed as you embark on this journey toward joy, peace, and contentment.

—Natalie Dawn Hanson, Speaker, Coach, Author of *Made to Soar: Christ-Centered Truths to Encourage, Equip, and Empower Moms* and Founder of the Made to Soar Movement.

The Joy Filled Soul

The Joy Filled Soul

Discover Peace and Contentment in Your Everyday

JANINE LANSING

Published by Author Academy Elite.
PO Box 43, Powell, OH 43065
authoracademyelite.com

All Scripture quotations, unless otherwise indicated, are from the
ESV® Bible (The Holy Bible, English Standard Version®),
Copyright © 2001 by Crossway, a publishing ministry of Good
News Publishers. Used by permission. All rights reserved.

Scripture quotations also taken from the New American Standard
Bible® (NASB), Copyright © 1960, 1962, 1963 1968, 1971, 1972,
1973, 1975, 1977, 1995 by The Lockman Foundation.
Used by permission. www.Lockman.org

ISBN: 978-1-64746-185-0 (Paperback)
ISBN: 978-1-64746-186-7 (Hardback)
ISBN: 978-1-64746-187-4 (eBook)

Library of Congress Control Number: 2020904723

*To the ladies in my life who compelled
me to love and forgive.*

contents

Introduction

I've got the joy, joy, joy, joy down in my heart, down in my heart to stay.[1]

I loved singing this song as a kid. We sang it often in our Sunday school class. No matter how I felt when the song started, I was certainly smiling by the end of the first verse. We would sing other verses too like the one that says "I've got the wonderful love of my blessed Redeemer way down in the depths of my heart." We'd sing it so fast and burst into laughter at the end. It really did bring happiness in the moment.

But as I've grown up, this song has become mysterious. It talks of having joy in my heart to stay, yet there are many times in life when I don't feel like I have joy in my heart. No matter how much I try to put it there to stay, it doesn't. Have you had similar experiences?

As I've grown in my relationship with Jesus and my knowledge of His Word, I've learned joy itself isn't the problem.

Joy was indeed designed to stay down in my heart. So, what caused it to vanish?

There's another song I learned growing up about a lady named Liza and a man named Henry. It begins: "There's a hole in my bucket, dear Liza, dear Liza. There's a hole in my bucket, dear Liza, a hole." [2] The song shares the whole story of Liza's suggestions to fix Henry's problem, but they come full circle as he ends up in the same place he started—with a hole in his bucket.

Joy couldn't stay in my heart because my heart was like Henry's bucket: it had a hole. I'm not talking about the need for salvation in Jesus (though that could also be described as a hole). After we've made the choice to trust in Jesus as our Savior and as we're working out our faith on a daily basis, there are times we choose joy only to turn around and find it gone. That's because there is a hole causing it to leak.

In the song Henry sets out on a quest to mend his bucket. Unfortunately for him there is no happy ending. It's rather a tragedy because he ends up in the same place he started. His bucket still has a hole.

This book will take us on a similar quest to find the holes causing our joy to leak out. Some holes will be huge, and we'll see joy gushing out in mere seconds. Others we'll find are slow leaks, draining the joy without us even noticing.

Unlike Henry, we will not end up in the same place we started. This book will be a journey for you and me to find ways to mend our holes. We'll walk through some of the dark, hard spaces and look intently at what is keeping joy from us, and then we'll explore truths found in the Scriptures that lead us to joy.

Many people before me have written about joy. The ideas and thoughts I present in this book are certainly not new ones because they are grounded in God's Word, which never changes. But perhaps these truths will be presented in a way you've never considered before. I aim to be practical so you may not simply read about joy but finally experience "the fullness of joy" (Psalm 16:11) that Jesus promises.

I have studied joy and experienced joy during some of the hardest, loneliest times in my life. I long to see my fellow sisters in Christ experience that same joy. Jesus gave it to every person who believes in Him. My purpose in this book is to remind you of that joy. Or maybe you're hearing about it for the first time. Either way, my deepest desire is that you will finally have joy down in your heart to stay.

May I pray for us as we begin this journey? Pray with me.

Dear God,
I want to thank You for my new friend, who is embarking on a journey to be filled with Your joy. I am so excited and honored to be her cheerleader—to guide, support, and encourage her along the way. I ask that You reveal Your truths through this book. I ask that You do not hesitate to point out the things in her life keeping her from experiencing joy in abundance. I also ask that You hold her gently through the process and mend her where she is most tender and broken.

Lord, You are kind and loving and gentle. I thank You for Your grace and mercy. Your loving-kindness is evident in my life, and my deepest desire is for it to be evident in my friend's life as well. I ask that You fill her with the knowledge of Your will with all spiritual wisdom and understanding so she may walk in a manner worthy of You, fully pleasing to You, being strengthened by Your glorious might that she may persevere and know Your true joy.

I thank You for being our sovereign God, who desperately wants a relationship with us, Your creation. And thank You for sending

Your Son to die in our place to ensure we can be together forever. May You bless this time we will spend together as we look into Your Word for guidance. Open our ears, our eyes, and our hearts. I ask this all in the powerful name of Jesus, Amen.

CHAPTER ONE

There's a Hole in My Cup

I remember the first time I had joy deep in my soul. I was in high school, and that particular day was very overwhelming and emotional. High school girls were not always nice. I knew I shouldn't care what the other girls thought about me because God loved me no matter what. But I couldn't figure out how I fit into the social scene there. On Tuesday I was accepted as part of the "in" crowd. But on Wednesday I was the subject of their gossip and laughter. I tried so hard to fit in. I wanted to be liked by everyone but always felt like I fell short of their acceptance.

That night I went outside and sat on the steps and stared up at the stars. The tears began to stream down my face, and I let them. I cried out to God and asked Him why. *Why is it so hard for me to make friends? Why are high school girls so mean? What is wrong with me?* I poured my heart out to God, searching for clarity and peace.

As I stared into the star-filled sky, I was lost. I didn't want to feel this way any longer. I didn't know what to do. Then a song came into my mind. It was a song I'd learned as a little kid from Psalty the Singing Songbook. It taught truths from 1 Peter 5:7. I began to sing aloud on the steps outside my house.

"I cast all my cares upon you. I lay all of my burdens down at your feet. And anytime I don't know what to do, I will cast all my cares upon you."[3]

I sang this song a few times, each time a little louder and with more resolve. And the more I sang, the more my soul was filled. It was filled with peace. It was filled with contentment. It was filled with certainty that God heard my cry and saw my tears. I had never felt anything like this so deep in my being.

It was joy. My soul was filling with joy, and the more I sang, the more it filled. It was a joy that didn't come from being accepted by my peers or having a best friend. It didn't come from laughter or happiness. It was a joy that came from deep inside, placed there by the God who created me with a purpose, who loves me unconditionally and genuinely cares about me. It was not a fleeting feeling. It was a deep, eternal, unwavering, untouchable joy that filled my soul.

And to think those days were simpler times! But they were. In my twenties joy was fickle. Sometimes I had it, and other times I didn't. It wasn't until I reached my thirties and discovered a newfound love of deeply studying God's Word that joy became more evident and more consistent in my life. I discovered truths about joy that transformed how I received and kept joy in my life.

What Joy Is and What Joy Isn't

Joy is a difficult word to define because there are very few synonyms for true joy. The dictionary says *joy* is "the emotion evoked by well-being, success, or good fortune or by the prospect of possessing what one desires; the state of happiness."[4] But this definition doesn't do the word justice. *Happiness* and *joy* are used interchangeably, yet *happy* seems a shallow synonym. I'd like to challenge this definition by explaining what joy is and what joy is not.

Joy Is Not an Emotion

First off, joy is not an emotion. Emotions are adjectives. They describe us. They help explain our current state. I am sad. He is mad. I am surprisingly calm in this moment.

Joy, however, is a noun. It is the state of being the emotions describe. We may feel happy when we have joy in the same way we may feel calm when we have peace. But peace and joy are states of being. They are static, even if our emotions change. Happy, sad, mad, angry, depressed, anxious, calm—those emotions fluctuate and are influenced by circumstances, medications, people, and many other things.

Emotions are fleeting and very temporal. I can be happy in one moment and the very next minute find myself contemplating the point of this life as I sit in depression. I can be calm with someone and then utterly enraged when they say something that upsets me. Why do I want to pursue happiness when it's only going to disappear? It's like I'm always chasing a high, and nothing seems to satisfy the craving for long.

Joy goes deeper. Joy isn't a mere blip on the radar that disappears shortly after making an appearance. Or, at least, it's not designed that way. True joy doesn't change with the tide. We expect joy to leave us like happiness does, but joy wasn't designed to leave us. Joy was designed to stay with us and to give us hope and encouragement throughout our day. It was designed to be a stabilizing force in our lives, not a fleeting emotion.

Joy Is a Perspective

We are going to encounter many situations in our lives. Some will bring happiness; some will bring sorrow. Some will bring anger, and some will bring despair. How do we face these situations? How do we interact with the trials set before us with peace and contentment? How do we fight the wars of this world without getting sucked into them?

In the book of Exodus, the Israelites wandered in the desert after God rescued them from Egypt. He caused the Red Sea to dry up so they could cross on dry land and escape their enemy. They had an opportunity to enter the land God promised them, yet they didn't. Why? Because their perspective was grounded in fear. They looked at the giants and trembled. They either didn't remember what God had done for them in Egypt and at the Red Sea, or they chose to forget. They got scared.

We will encounter big and scary things in our lives, most of which will be out of our control. We will have to face them regardless if we want to or not. Having a perspective of joy instead of fear will affect the outcome.

The moment we wake up, we decide how we will approach our day. Will we go through our day dreading it, or will we make it the best it can be?

I once asked my friend, "Do you see the glass half full or half empty?"

She replied, "I'm just grateful I have a cup."

We have choices as to how to live our lives. Is your glass half empty? Is your glass half full? Or are you simply grateful you have a cup?

Winston Churchill once said, "A pessimist sees the difficulty in every opportunity. An optimist sees the opportunity in every difficulty."[5] Joy doesn't change our circumstance. But it can change us! Do you ever wonder how two people can go through the same situation and come out completely different?

There's a story that tells of an egg, a potato, and some coffee beans. Have you heard it? A father wanted to teach his daughter a life lesson, so he put three pots of water on the stove to boil. To one he adds an egg. To another he adds a potato. And to the last he adds some coffee beans.

After some minutes had passed, he asked his daughter to touch the potato, crack the egg, and drink the coffee. He then explained that the potato, the egg, and the coffee beans had each faced the same adversity—the boiling water. However, each reacted differently.

The potato went in strong, hard, and unrelenting, but in boiling water it became soft and weak. The egg was fragile with the thin shell protecting its liquid interior until it was put in the boiling water. Then the inside of the egg hardened. But the coffee beans were unique. After they were exposed to the boiling water, they changed the water and created something new.

Joy is like the coffee beans. As we enter situations, both difficult and easy, joy has the potential not only to change us, but it can also change the situation, much like the coffee beans changed the water. If we have joy, it will alter how we see life, how we interact with life. Joy is the perspective with which we approach and interact with our circumstances.

Joy Is Not a Choice—It's a Result of Our Choices

Almost everywhere I go, I see signs or hear people encouraging one another to "choose joy." I even have a water bottle with those words printed on the side. It's fair to say we can choose happiness. But choose joy? It's not that simple.

It's more accurate to say joy is a result of our choices, not the choice itself. If I want to be healthy, I will eat whole foods and exercise. I will choose to eat a carrot rather than a slice of cake. I will choose to go for a walk rather than sit and watch television. Being healthy is a result of the choices we make. Simply stating "I choose to be healthy" won't make you healthy. The choice that must be made isn't to be healthy. One must choose whether to eat whole foods and exercise or eat cake and skip exercise.

Similarly, stating "I choose joy" won't give you joy. We can try all we want, but joy is a result of our good choices, not the choice itself.

I must make choices that support my pursuit of joy. If I long for joy, then I choose to be kind because that brings joy into my life. But if I long for joy and choose to cut someone off on the freeway, then I can't expect joy to follow. You can say you "choose joy" all day long, but if you are being mean to someone, joy won't come. Bitterness and anger will come instead. But if I choose to be kind, then joy and peace and contentment will result.

I realized something while I sat on those steps outside my house. I was not filled with joy because of who I was or anything I had done. I wasn't filled with joy because I chose to be. I was filled with joy because my gaze was fixed on Jesus. When I went outside, I was focused on myself, but something changed when I started to sing. My focus switched from myself and my circumstances to Jesus and His promises. I chose to worship Jesus. And joy came as a result of that choice.

That is the foundation of this book. The following chapters will discuss several choices that, if made correctly, will support our pursuit for joy and mend our cups.

My Cup

My youngest child has always been a lover of chocolate milk. When she was four, she decided she was old enough to get it herself. I watched her move a chair all over the kitchen as she gathered the necessary ingredients. She then filled her cup, but she didn't stop as the milk neared the top. She kept pouring. The milk spilled onto the counter before she stopped.

God desires the same for us. Picture your soul as the cup and God's joy as the chocolate milk. He wants to pour and pour and pour, continuing even as He nears the top. He wants it to overflow.

The soul is the very breath of life. Genesis tells the story of how God created man.

> Then the LORD God formed man of dust from the ground and breathed into his nostrils the breath of life, and the man became a living *creature*" (emphasis mine).
>
> —Genesis 2:7

The word *creature* is the Hebrew word *nephesh*[6] and is most often translated as *soul.* Man became a living *soul.*

We are living, breathing, physical beings capable of feeling and doing and living. Our souls are not the spiritual part of us, separate from the physical body. We don't have souls; we are souls. You've heard the phrase "She's an old soul." This is said of someone identified as wiser and more mature than her biological age. You may have also heard the phrase "She's a beautiful soul." My prayer is that when someone speaks about you, they'll say, "She's a joy-filled soul."

7

My Cup Overflows

I have struggled through painful friendships, medical issues, accusations, betrayal, and many nights of wondering why life had to be so cruel. In those moments I've struggled to remember that I have a purpose and that I am loved. Some days are harder than others. Some days I let anger, bitterness, and pride corrupt my thoughts. Some days I get caught up with the chaos of this life and forget my eternal perspective. And those are the days that my joy begins to leak. But deep down I know the truth: God created me for a purpose and walks with me every day.

> The LORD is my shepherd; I shall not want. He makes me lie down in green pastures. He leads me beside still waters. He restores my soul. He leads me in paths of righteousness for his name's sake. Even though I walk through the valley of the shadow of death, I will fear no evil, for you are with me; your rod and your staff, they comfort me. You prepare a table before me in the presence of my enemies; you anoint my head with oil; my cup overflows. Surely goodness and mercy shall follow me all the days of my life, and I shall dwell in the house of the LORD forever.
>
> —Psalm 23

I memorized this Psalm in kindergarten, but it wasn't until recently as an adult that I really understood how much promise fills this passage. It embodies joy, a joy that in the presence of my enemies reminds me I am not alone. God is protecting me. He is all I need. He is enough. God brings comfort and peace when chaos is swarming around me. He brings reassurance that He still has a plan for my life, even when issues and situations seem to sing a different song. He restores my soul and fills it with joy. My cup overflows.

Thinking back to those high school days again, having a perspective of joy did not make the girls nicer. It didn't stop them from talking about me behind my back. It didn't keep the tears from falling down my face. It didn't change my sadness into happiness. But joy brought me hope. It brought me peace. It helped me become confident in who I was. My identity was rooted in the joy of the Lord, and that joy told me everything was going to be okay and that I was okay. I didn't need to be anyone else or anything else. I needed to be Janine, the person God created to be filled with His joy and bring Him glory. Joy brought contentment.

Who are you today? What are you facing? Are you allowing the circumstances you're facing to become your identity? Are you allowing your emotions to determine your peace? Are you allowing other people to dictate how you feel about life? Are you "choosing joy," but it doesn't last?

If you answered yes to any of these questions, you are not alone. And I'm glad you're here. In my introduction to this book, I told the story of Henry and the hole in his bucket. Henry had to fix the bucket before he could fill it with water. And fixing the bucket wasn't easy. He had many obstacles in his path. In the end his quest was futile, and he found himself in the same sorry position he began. We won't.

My hope is that the next few chapters will help you identify what is allowing your cup to leak and give you steps to mend your soul and fill it with joy. There may be holes in your cup right now, but we are on our way to being mended with purpose and having a joy-filled soul.

CHAPTER TWO
The Secret Ingredient

My mom loves to cook and bake. She made cinnamon rolls the other day for her adult fellowship class, and everyone raved that these were the best cinnamon rolls they'd ever eaten. And they've eaten their fair share of cinnamon rolls. So, what made these the best?

It could simply be that my mom is a really good baker. It could be that she used the perfect combination of spices. It could be that she proofed the dough perfectly to get the rise just right. Though all these factors might have influenced the outcome, the real reason they were better than any other was the secret ingredient: Yukon potatoes.

There is a secret ingredient to true, lasting joy. It will make our joy the best we've ever had, much like those cinnamon rolls. That secret ingredient is . . . drum roll, please . . . Jesus. Okay so I'm sure most of you guessed that answer because it's really not a secret at all. Some of you didn't give it a second thought because you've heard it before. But I want to challenge us to deeply consider true joy and where it comes from. Sometimes when we've believed something for a while, our attitude becomes lazy, apathetic, even watered down.

That's what happened to me. I grew up in the church and studied the Bible in various capacities all my life. I studied the fruit of the Spirit numerous times as well as the book of Philippians (known as the "Book of Joy"). So, when I found myself struggling to keep joy in my life, I thought it was normal, simply part of the Christian experience.

I was invited to do a study on David when I was in my late twenties. It was the deepest, hardest study I'd ever done, but that study rocked my world. It transformed my thinking. It brought Jesus back to the forefront of my mind. I began to experience a relationship with Jesus, an intimacy with Jesus, as I never had before.

Through that study on David, I discovered that an intimate relationship with Jesus is foundational to real, unfaltering joy. It's not enough to believe. It's in His presence that we find fullness of joy. David writes about this in Psalm 16. He doesn't say "a little bit of joy" or "some joy." David says, "In [God's] presence there is *fullness* of joy" (emphasis mine). You want a cup overflowing with joy? It starts with Jesus. It begins with the God who created you.

God with Us

In the beginning God walked with Adam and Eve in the garden. When sin entered the picture, that intimacy with God disappeared. God never abandoned His people, but He couldn't interact with them in the way He originally designed. He is holy and due to sin, mankind is not.

As believers in Jesus, we are the closest mankind has been to God since Adam and Eve walked with Him in the garden because we have the Holy Spirit living in us. He's not in a box or behind a curtain like He was for the Israelites in the Old Testament. He dwells in us. He's with us twenty-four hours a day, seven days a week.

Jesus told His disciples there would be sorrow. He warned them so they wouldn't be surprised or overwhelmed or drown in their grief. He wouldn't be there as a shoulder to cry on. So, He gave them something that would carry them through the difficulty. He offered them His joy—His complete joy in each of them through the Holy Spirit. And the same is offered to us as believers today.

If the God who created me wants to give me His joy, why am I not embracing it? What is keeping me from it? Why am I turning to other sources to find joy and comfort?

I do this all the time. When I've had a really, really bad day, all I want is to sit down, eat some junk food, and watch a movie. Is it only me, or have you been there? I grab a brownie or a bag of chips and head for the couch. I reason it away, telling myself, *I've had a really bad day, and I deserve it.* But God is saying, "No, you need me. In those moments when life is hard, I'm the answer. I will bring you more joy than that brownie or movie ever will." Jesus wants to bring us comfort. The Holy Spirit is already living in us to give us joy.

The world says happiness is out there to find. It also says we need to discover who we are so we can bring ourselves happiness. Ladies, we can't bring ourselves happiness. We can search our entire lives for something out there to bring us satisfaction, but the truth is that if we know Jesus, we've already found it. We don't have to search anywhere else. We must simply turn to Jesus, to His truth, and accept it. And if that's difficult to do, we need to tell Him and sit with Him through the uncertainty.

God has done everything to be present with me and to give me His joy. I am not going to squash it. I'm not going to render it useless. I will honor His presence by fully embracing His joy.

Abide with Him

Joy is possible because of Jesus. He said, "These things I have spoken to you, that my joy may be in you, and that your joy may be full" (John 15:11). In the previous verses of this chapter, Jesus tells His disciples to abide in Him and His love and to keep His commandments. So, how do we overflow our cups with Jesus's joy?

Abide in Him. *Abide* means to "dwell" and to "continue to be in a place for a significant amount of time, to linger."[7]

I have two types of friends: my coffee friends and my walking friends. Let me explain. Every day I walk my kids to school. Sometimes we end up walking at the same time as some other families. I chitchat with the mom about the weather or the rush to get out the door. Sometimes we go a little deeper and talk about sicknesses or the crazy weekend we had. I know some intimate details about their life, but not many. These are my walking friends.

Then I have my coffee friends. These are the friends I sit down with over coffee or a meal and hear more about their lives. I know more about their kids and what they like to do. I hear the heartaches, and I pray with them. They listen to me, and they are genuinely interested in my family too. I linger with these friends.

Here's my question. When was the last time you lingered with Jesus? Is He your walking friend or your coffee friend? Is He the one you chitchat with for a few quick moments in the morning or night? Or is He the one you linger with and share intimate details? If we don't abide with Jesus, then the joy He desires to give us will never fully be ours.

His Joy Is Ours

My daughter recently received a slap bracelet. It's a little animal that wraps around her wrist. She put it on and repeatedly pushed the "Try Me" button. When she did, the tiny animal made a squeak that made her laugh. She loved it, but she didn't realize the animal did much more than make a funny sound. Once we pulled the tab and disconnected the "Try Me" button, she realized the animal talked too. We released the toy to do everything it was made to do.

If you believe in Jesus, if you've confessed with your mouth that Jesus is Lord, and if you believe in your heart God raised Him from the dead, you are saved (Romans 10:9-10). At that moment, the Holy Spirit came to live in you, to guide you, and to intercede for you. He gives every believer the gift of unconditional joy.

Romans 15:13 says, "May the God of hope fill you with all joy and peace in believing, so that by the power of the Holy Spirit you may abound in hope." If we simply trust Jesus and don't allow the Spirit to work in our lives, it's like putting the slap bracelet on our wrist with the "try me" button still attached. But if we allow the Holy Spirit to move and release His power, our joy will overflow. When we allow the Holy Spirit to transform our lives, we release joy to do everything it was designed to do.

God will fill us with joy and peace as we believe in Him. It's a continuous belief. It's active and ongoing. It's a relationship. It's a giving of our entire selves to Jesus. And in return, we will abound with hope because of the Holy Spirit's power. We have hope in every situation because of joy.

What does that look like? What does it look like to give our everything to Jesus? In the church we often use the term *surrender*, but I always think of surrender as waving the white flag. God doesn't want us to wave the white flag. We're on the same team.

Then what does surrender really look like? Remember, our soul is everything. When we become one with Jesus, when we know Jesus intimately, it includes our thoughts, our emotions, our desires. Surrendering is becoming one with Jesus and wanting His will instead of ours.

I married my husband, Tim, in 2004. We became one as the Bible talks about, but it takes time and effort to truly become one. Even now we often have differing opinions on issues, and this can cause conflict. This becomes evident in raising our four kids. I want to do it this way. He wants to do it differently. We've learned that communication with each other and God is essential. We pray for guidance and discernment, and then we discuss the issue. Sometimes I go his way, sometimes he comes my way, and sometimes we compromise.

Our relationship with Jesus should be no different, except His way is always the right way. As much as I may think my way is always right, it's not. Jesus is always right. No compromise is needed, but conversation is still an essential part of the surrender puzzle.

Surrender is not waving the white flag. It's trusting God's will, knowing He has my growth in mind. When I don't agree with God, I talk with Him about it as I would talk with Tim when I don't agree on something in our marriage. It's okay to ask questions of the Lord. That's good communication.

Surrender is inviting Jesus into the relationship we say we have. It's becoming one with Him. The longer I'm married to Tim, the more I enjoy our conversations and even our disagreements. I know him better and can even predict what he wants, what he'll say, and how he will respond in a certain situation. Our relationship with Jesus should be no different. The more time I spend with Him, the more I'm likely to understand His will.

Not My Will, But Yours Be Done

Moments before Jesus was arrested and sentenced to death, He prayed to His Father.

"Father, if you are willing, remove this cup from me. Nevertheless, not my will, but yours, be done." And there appeared to him an angel from heaven, strengthening him. And being in agony he prayed more earnestly; and his sweat became like great drops of blood falling down to the ground.

—Luke 22:42-44

At this moment, Jesus in His humanity sought an alternative plan for our redemption. Knowing He was about to be tortured and crucified, He asked His Father if there was another way. Jesus desired the same outcome as His Father. He was willing to die and He wanted to fulfill the law and pay our debt.

Yet He prayed three times that the Father would "remove this cup" from Him. He was honest with Him. He shared His thoughts and desires with Him. And ultimately became the perfect example of surrender. Not my will, but Yours, be done.

So, what does surrender look like for us? Four areas call for our surrender: our desires, our thoughts, our emotions, and our actions.

Our Desires

A *desire* is something we long for or hope for. It's a "conscious impulse"[8] toward something. When our desires are met, there is often a sense of satisfaction or enjoyment, though it may be temporary. That is why desires are hard to ignore and even harder to surrender.

Some of our desires are godly, some are sinful, and some are neutral. Some are silly while others impact eternity. We can desire something to eat or consume. We can desire entertainment. We can also desire another person's things or job or spouse. Our desires can get us into a lot of trouble, or they can bring us closer to God.

Psalm 37:4 says, "Delight yourself in the LORD, and he will give you the desires of your heart." That's not to say all my desires will come true if I delight in the Lord. It means that when we delight in the Lord, when we find our joy in Him and abide in Him, our desires will conform to His.

I had a roommate in college I connected with super well. The more we hung out, the more we grew alike. By the end of the year, our cycles were the same. Our wardrobes looked the same. We even started to talk like each other. She picked up my quirks, and I picked up hers. Similarly, when we spend time with Jesus, our desires become like His. Our speech becomes like His. Our thoughts become like His.

If you're at all like me, there are times when you may not know or understand your deepest desires. We need to ask ourselves and God why we do certain things and have certain desires. Answering this question often directs us to a state of longing for security, significance, and a place to belong. Unfortunately, we may look to fulfill these desires in the wrong places. Surrendering our desires doesn't automatically mean giving up on our dreams, but it does mean trusting Jesus to fulfill our desires in His timing and His way.

Remember, Jesus had a different desire than God the Father before He died on the cross. His desire, His request, was for the Father to find another way. Yet, when it came down to it, He surrendered His desire and fulfilled the will of the Father.

Invite God into the conversation. Ask Him to show you when your desires are focused on false sources of satisfaction. If our desires are self-seeking and self-glorifying rather than glorifying to God, those are the desires we need to let go. But we don't have to figure it out on our own. Through abiding in Jesus and being honest with Him about your desires, He will make it clear which desires need to be given up or altered and which ones align with His will.

Our Thoughts

Thoughts cover a lot of ground. They can be thoughts we have about ourselves. They can be thoughts we have about others. They can be the plans we make, the dreams we have.

Let's start with the thoughts we have about ourselves and others. When we surrender our thoughts, we acknowledge that sometimes our thoughts are based on truths and sometimes on lies. The only way to know which is the case is to hold them up to God's Word.

Sometimes I experience intrusive thoughts. For example: *I could never write a book. I don't have anything worthwhile to say. No one cares about what I think.* When this happens, I hold those thoughts up to Scripture and see if they hold true. And guess what? They don't.

The Scriptures say we are a body, and I need to do my part (Romans 12). Each one of us has a different part to play with different skills and gifts (1 Corinthians 12), and I need to use mine to glorify God (1 Peter 4). He created me for a purpose (Ephesians 2), and I am to shine Jesus to the world (Matthew 5).

This same process should apply when I think about someone else. I remember every single person is made in the image of God. If I think poorly about someone else, I am sinning against that person and God, who created them.

I am a thinker. My husband would say I think too much. My mind is constantly running, and much of what I think about is how I can improve something or plans I have for the future. When I think of surrendering my thoughts, sometimes I rejoice in it because I simply want my brain to stop thinking. However, other times I have a great idea, and I don't want to give that up.

I've learned that surrender doesn't mean giving up our plans and ideas. Some of those plans and ideas were given to you by God Himself. By checking in with Him, asking for His guidance and insight, and making sure that the idea is coming from Him—that's surrender.

Jesus sent us a helper: the Holy Spirit. But sometimes we forget to let Him help us. As believers we have the Holy Spirit living in us. He will nudge us and make us aware if things aren't right. The Holy Spirit bridges the gap between the things of God and our soul so we may understand His Word (1 Corinthians 2:6-10).

So, when it comes time to make the decision to implement a plan, you should have peace. If you don't have peace, it may be a nudge from the Holy Spirit that something is off, that something needs to change. This happens through prayer, study of His Word, and consultation with godly people.

Our Emotions

Most people who know me would say I'm an emotional person. Growing up, teachers and coaches often told me to stop crying and that I was too emotional. It made me feel horrible. I believed something was wrong with me. I believed God created me as an emotional being, but the authority figures in my life told me my emotions were bad. I couldn't reconcile the two conflicting views.

I learned to control my tears and hide them. I was told to "suck it up," so I did. But hiding our feelings is not what surrendering our emotions is all about. We don't have to give up our emotions or hide them to follow Jesus. Quite the opposite. Feelings are so much a part of us. Our emotions are more tightly woven to our identity than our thoughts. Dan Allender and Tremper Longman III speak of this in *The Cry of the Soul.* They write that "emotions are the language of the soul" and state, ". . . ignoring our emotions is turning our back on reality . . . In neglecting our intense emotions, we are false to ourselves and lose a wonderful opportunity to know God."[9] We can't afford to ignore our emotions or hide them. We must share them with Jesus.

As I cried on those steps that day in high school, my intimacy with God was an intense experience, something I had never experienced before. What was different? I was honest with how I felt, and I invited God into the process. I didn't hide it. I didn't ask Him to make it go away. I shared with Him and allowed Him to sit with me.

When we talk about surrendering our emotions, we need to remember our emotions are developed within a context. I remember getting upset with a fellow student while I was in grad school. He always seemed to drop the ball when we worked on a project together. I remember confronting him about it in anger. It was not my finest moment. He then told me that his mom had stage IV cancer; that he was taking care of his four siblings; and that two of them had been throwing up for the past two days.

The context of my emotions changed. He wasn't slacking in his responsibility to the project because he was lazy, which was what I thought. He was slacking because he had bigger, more important concerns at that time.

My emotions changed from anger to compassion because I had the correct context. As we surrender our emotions to Jesus, a biblical context is critical. Emotions aren't bad. They are a gift from God. And we don't have to give them up. But we do need to make sure they align with Jesus and conform to the truth of Scripture.

Our Actions

What am I going to do today? Where will I go, and how will I spend my time? Every day we can choose what we will do with the precious hours given to us.

Surrendering my actions means I will be a good steward of my time. I will make conscious choices regarding how I spend my day. Every action we take serves somebody. It may serve others. It may serve God. It may serve ourselves. When we surrender our actions, we ask ourselves, "Whom will I serve today?"

How I treat people through my actions will be a big indicator of whom I serve and to whom I've surrendered. When I treat my kids as if they are a nuisance, I'm serving myself, and my actions show it. But when I treat my kids with kindness and tenderness, with love, I'm serving God and them, and my actions show it.

Psalm 46:10a says, "Be still, and know that I am God." The same verse in the New American Standard Bible opens with "cease striving." Sometimes surrendering our actions means we simply need to stop. Cease striving. Cease doing. If you don't know whether your actions are in line with God's, stop, ask Him, and then wait for His response.

Lifetime Warranty

As we linger with Jesus and develop an intimate relationship with Him, our cups are mended, and our joy overflows. Things and situations threaten our joy every day: comparison, anxiety, disappointment, and conflict. These puncture our cup and allow our joy to leak. But Jesus can mend those holes.

Not only does He mend them, He gives us a lifetime warranty on His work. Let's face it. We surrender on Sunday, but on Monday we're back to trusting our desires, thoughts, and emotions. Our God offers a lifetime warranty. He promises to mend our cup every single time we surrender.

I bought a set of pans when I was newly married. They had a lifetime warranty. In the beginning I always washed them by hand because we didn't have a dishwasher. When we finally bought a dishwasher, I was so excited to use it, so I put my pans in there to see if it could clean them too. When I took the pans out, the non-stick coating began to peel. I called the company to get them replaced, and they asked if I put the pans in the dishwasher. I told them I had. They told me my lifetime warranty was no longer valid. Putting my pans in the dishwasher voided my warranty.

Nothing we can do will void our lifetime warranty with Jesus. When we take back control and trust our desires, thoughts, or emotions instead of Jesus, it doesn't void the warranty. Even if the holes we've created have been mended one hundred times before, Jesus will still mend our souls.

If your cup is chipped or even shattered, Jesus can mend it. He doesn't only mend holes; He picks up the broken and shattered pieces of our lives and makes us whole. We say, "Not my will but Yours be done," and He mends our cups and then fills them with joy. It's truly a beautiful picture.

CHAPTER THREE

When You Wish upon A...

Have you ever thought at least one of the following statements?

I wish I had her hair. I wish I could be brave like her. I wish I had a boyfriend or a husband. I wish I had a more fulfilling job. I wish I had less stress. I wish I wasn't sick.

I've thought all of these at some point in my life. And I could probably fill this entire chapter with more wishes. When I was in high school, every person around me had a date for the winter formal except me. I wanted to wish upon a star and make it happen. If only that would work.

One of the songs popular on country radio at the time was "Someone Else's Star" by Bryan White.[10] He wishes for someone to love, and he sees wishes coming true for others. He concludes that because his wishes aren't coming true, he must be wishing on "someone else's star." This song played on repeat in my room. I laid in bed, wishing I was prettier, wishing a boy would like me, wishing for so many things I didn't really need but my teenage heart desired.

I'm so grateful now that my wishes didn't come true the way I wanted. Of course, God's plan for my life and who I would date and marry were way better than I could have ever imagined.

Over the years, I've wished for more things. I wished to get pregnant, wished to get my dream job, and wished for friendships. The trouble with wishes is that they can quickly become discontentment without us realizing it. And discontentment is the number one reason we lack joy. When we wish, we become unsatisfied with where we are, what we have, who we're with, how we look, or what we do. And in this society where pleasing self and being satisfied is of utmost importance, we naturally are distressed when satisfaction is missing.

Wishing Well

We were designed with desire. There are so many things in life that dissatisfy us and interrupt our contentment – more than we can discuss in this chapter. But there are a few "wishes" that have been the biggest causes of holes in my cup, and I'm thinking I'm not alone in these desires. It might have something to do with where "me" lands in the sentence we're telling ourselves.

Wishing "Me" Had What You Have

Life is all about comparison. From the minute we're born, people start comparing us to one another. She looks more like her mom than her dad. She's not as chubby as her sister was. He's so little compared to his brother. I heard all these comments when my kids were born. It is almost impossible to escape the comparison game we play with each other. We compare vacation spots, the number of kids we have, house sizes, the cleanliness of our houses, incomes, styles or fashions, jobs, and pretty much anything else you can think of. In this mode of competition, we tirelessly aim to one-up or outdo one another. On social media this competition is amplified. She has more followers than me, or his picture received more likes than mine. We even get competitive with our hardships. My kid has more allergies than yours, or my pain is worse than yours. It's a never-ending trap we have set for ourselves.

I remember going on Facebook the day after Thanksgiving last year. I was bombarded by posts from all my mom friends. They were posting their first day photos of either advent activities or Elf on the Shelf. I, of course, had nothing planned for my kids.

In that moment I felt like the worst mom in the world, as if I had failed them in some way. I have a running joke with my husband that when I make a mistake, I say, "hashtag mom fail 2,367." I'm not actually keeping count, but sometimes it feels like I've failed a million times and then some. But did I really fail because I didn't do advent with my kids? Of course not.

How about you? What is your comparison trap? Maybe you're confident in who you are, but you find yourself envious of what others have, like their house or job. Or maybe the envy comes from wishing you had someone else's family or social life. Anytime you think "I have (blank)" followed by "They have (blank)", you are playing the dangerous game of comparison.

Even in our hardships, this can happen. We either downplay our own struggles because they are not as severe as another's, or we contend that we always get the shortest lot. And somehow we feel better because we're suffering more than someone else. This is simply not true. Our struggles are different. If one involves less sorrow than another, that doesn't invalidate the struggle. Likewise, just because a struggle is less significant by the world's standards, that doesn't make the struggle easier.

I admit I've done this numerous times. My body becomes easily inflamed due to autoimmune conditions, causing great pain. When I hear my husband say his back hurts, empathy isn't the first thing that naturally comes to my mind. If I'm honest, the first thought usually is "You have no idea what pain is." I belittle his pain because I'm focused on myself.

As I've grown in Jesus, thoughts like that are less and less frequent only because of the Lord's intervention in my heart. I naturally compare my life with others, even the hardships, and when I do, discontentment creeps in.

Wishing "Me" Was Somewhere Else

I have always dreamed of living outside of California. I was convinced I would go away to college. I only had out-of-state schools on my list. But plans changed when things started getting serious with this guy I was dating. I decided to stay local, and four years later we were married. The itch to live somewhere else, however, never went away.

I've had countless conversations with Tim about where I've dreamed of living. Washington and Colorado have always topped my list. As we've traveled to new places, I've added more places to my list. So, when Tim received a job offer in Indiana, I thought for sure this was the answer to my prayers.

Many people asked, "Why would you want to trade sunny Southern California for Indiana?" I responded, "I'm a country girl at heart trapped in the city. I long for acreage, not square footage. I dream of living in a place with wide-open spaces and four seasons."

But the underlying truth was that I was not content with my circumstances. Everywhere else looked better than where I was. You know the saying "the grass is always greener on the other side." I thought that was true. I thought the grass was greener somewhere else. I looked and even prayed for a change. So, when the job offer came, I wanted to jump at the opportunity. But my husband did not. He declined the position because he felt it wasn't a good fit for him or us.

A couple years later an offer presented itself in Ohio. I was hopeful again. But he turned that one down too. I prayed daily, asking God to move us somewhere else. I waited patiently, doing all the right things. Or so I thought.

Then I realized while doing a deep dive study in the book of Philippians that God was asking me to be content where I was, where He had planted me.

I had always thought contentment had to do with things. I was satisfied and content with *what we had*, but I realized that day I wasn't content with *where we were*.

"I have learned the secret of facing plenty and hunger, abundance and need" (Philippians 4:12b). Paul the apostle was in prison when he wrote those words. I'm sure he desired to move from his current location even more than I wanted to move from mine. Yet he did not direct his prayers that way. He was content with where he was.

That realization felt like a punch to the gut. I was crazy convicted.

Discontentment comes from our dissatisfaction with our circumstances. For me it was my location. What is it for you? What dissatisfies you? Is it your job? Your relationship (or lack thereof)? Your income?

Being satisfied in whatever situation you are in because you are satisfied in Him is what God desires for us.

Wishing "Me" Had More Time for Me

There is a huge movement right now for self-care. I get it. We're tired and overextended. I'm crankier and more irritable when I'm stressed. If I take some time for myself, I won't be as stressed or irritable, and therefore I can love my family better.

Some of this self-care movement is coming from a good place. We do need to take care of ourselves. We need to eat healthy foods, move our bodies, take care of our mental health, and control the thoughts that come and go through our mind.

God Himself reserved a day of rest after creating the world. Genesis 2:2-3 records that on day seven He rested. As a mama of four, I crave rest. So, this "take time for me" idea is extremely attractive. But if I may be so bold, I'd like to share something that is even more refreshing and rejuvenating than time to myself. It's time in God's Word.

If we're going to implement "self-care," it must include spiritual health, not only physical and mental health. Going to the spa, taking a nap, getting a pedicure, and shopping by myself is not going to give me what I really need to love others. We say we're doing these things so we can have the space and capacity to love others better. But we love because God loved us first. We love others better when we spend time with Him.

It's fine to go get the pedicure and to go shopping without your kids. There is nothing like going through the aisles at Target without little hands grabbing everything and little mouths asking, "Can I have that?" at every turn. Rest, enjoy God's goodness, and have time by yourself. But if you are taking time for yourself because you are struggling to love others, if your joy is lacking and you don't feel you have anything to give, then spending time in God's Word will be more beneficial than that pedicure.

Wishing "Me" Was Liked by Everyone

I have many conversations with myself, sometimes daily, reminding my heart and mind that the opinions of others are inconsequential, that all that matters is how God feels about me. This is hardest when I feel judged by others. My husband doesn't care if others are judging him. I don't know if it's because I'm a woman or if it's because of my personality, but I really want to meet other people's expectations. I want to please them.

The tricky part is that there is a longing and desire to belong, to have purpose, inside each one of us. God planted purpose within each of us during creation. We're also made to worship something. Because of this, if we're not worshipping God, we're going to worship something else. Some worship money. Some worship the next high. Some worship power and position.

When I desire to please others, I'm worshipping approval. I'm doing everything in my life to gain acceptance. I'm changing who I am, what I say, how I dress, what I'm involved in, and so much more to fit what I think others expect of me so I can feel secure and significant.

Wishing for True Contentment

Is true contentment possible? Can I really be satisfied where I am in my current circumstances? Can I be content with who I am and not desire to be anyone or anything else? The Bible tells us it's possible. We don't have to wish for it. Paul was able to find contentment while in prison (Philippians 4). We don't know for sure which prison he was in or what the conditions were like, but we can make a few guesses. It is likely he was under house arrest at the time. So, he could have visitors, but he couldn't go out. He had already been on at least three missionary journeys and now found himself unable to travel. That probably bummed him out a bit.

He also couldn't do his job the way he was used to doing it. He couldn't plant churches or encourage believers except through letters. He had to evangelize and disciple people within the confines of his new limitations. He certainly wasn't building any tents. He probably didn't have much privacy either. Yet, he learned contentment and joy. If he could be content in his circumstances, then we can too.

Here are six suggestions that can help us find true contentment without wishing for more wishes.

Reset Your Focus

The grass is always greener on the other side. But what if it's not true? What if the grass is only greener on the other side because you don't water your own lawn? What if your grass is dead because you're focusing on the wrong thing? When we are constantly focused on what *we* want God to do or what *we* want from Him, what *we* think is best for our lives, we miss the amazing things He has planned for us. Instead, if we focus on God and what *He* desires and what *He* is trying to teach us, we'll find our satisfaction in Him.

A popular mantra out there says, "Be true to yourself." The idea is that it doesn't matter what anyone else says. You need to do what you feel is right without compromise. While I agree we shouldn't care what other people think, and we definitely should not compromise our values, the problem with this ideal is the focus on me and my desires. And here's the truth: what I feel is right might be very wrong.

When we focus on ourselves and what is "best" or "true" for us, we take God out of the picture. Ladies, we can't afford to do that. We need to focus on Christ, not ourselves. You don't want me to be true to myself. I am a sinner. I am angry, irritable, selfish, proud, etc. If I'm true to myself, then I will demand my way every time.

But if my focus switches from being true to myself and instead looks intently on God and His Word, my grass suddenly doesn't seem so bad, and contentment is easier to find.

Paul understood this concept. It was for the sake of Christ that he contented himself in all circumstances.

Three times I pleaded with the Lord about this [thorn], that it should leave me. But he said to me, "My grace is sufficient for you, for my power is made perfect in weakness." Therefore I will boast all the more gladly of my weaknesses, so that the power of Christ may rest upon me. For the sake of Christ, then, I am content with weaknesses, insults, hardships, persecutions, and calamities. For when I am weak, then I am strong.

—2 Corinthians 12:8-10

So, how do we put our focus on Jesus? We listen to His wisdom through the Bible. The more I read God's Word and sit with Him, the more I desire what He desires, and joy abounds. When we focus on God, we begin to see our lives from His perspective and His truth. Then the neighbor's grass doesn't matter anymore.

Know Your Why

When we aren't satisfied with where we are, who we're with, or what we do, it's usually because we don't know our "why." When we don't know our why, we look to ourselves for the answer, or we turn to others to tell us who we are.

We need to know our why. Why do you get up each morning? Why do you do what you do? If you don't know the answers to these questions, you will always look to others for the answers. I've found that the confident women in my life are not confident because of their personality; it comes from their relationship with God. They know who they are in Christ, and it's enough. They don't need anyone else's approval.

33

Paul knew his why. He knew that everything he did was to bring glory to God and to bring people to Him. Paul says, "For to me to live is Christ, and to die is gain" (Philippians 1:21). Paul knew his whole purpose was to advance the kingdom of God. And if he were to die, it would be okay because he would finally be in Jesus's presence. Paul knew his why, and it led to his contentment.

Quiet the Lies

Turn off as many comparison traps as possible. Some will always be present, but if you can step away or eliminate a trap or two, then do it. If you know you struggle with comparison on social media, then don't go there. Quiet the naysayers and the people who try to change your why.

You might think so-and-so's opinion about you matters, so you should change who you are or what you are doing because they don't like it. Well, that lie needs to go. If I'm honest, there are times I find myself thinking similar thoughts all day long. But I know who I am because I know the God who made me. I don't simply know *of* Him. I know *Him* intimately. So, the lies in my head need to hit the road.

One of my favorite things to do is climb into a canoe, paddle out into the middle of a quiet lake, and sit there. I put the oar across the canoe, and dragonflies land on the end. Only when a dragonfly lands on the lake instead of my oar is the water disturbed. That tiny movement causes ripples to echo across the lake, traveling across the surface.

The lies in our lives have a ripple effect like the dragonfly on a quiet lake. Quieting these lies is so important because they reach far past our initial thought. They end up altering our actions for the day or even months later.

Have you heard someone say you just need to love yourself? While I can appreciate where the advocates of this motto are coming from, the "love yourself" lifestyle is another lie. It stems from the commandment that Jesus gives in three of the gospels (Matthew 22, Mark 12, Luke 10) to "love your neighbor as yourself." It's also found in the Old Testament (Leviticus 19), and Paul refers to Jesus's commandment in Galatians 5 as well.

Notice Jesus didn't say, "Love your neighbor *and* yourself" or "Love your neighbor *after* yourself." He said, "Love your neighbor *as* yourself." We will always watch out for number one, ourselves. Jesus was challenging His followers to make our neighbor our number one instead. The desires we have for ourselves should be our desires for our neighbor. If my coworker gets a raise or my neighbor gets a new car, I should be excited for them as I hope they would be for me. Unfortunately, we often want the best for ourselves and hope for the worst for others, especially our enemies.

The world tells us that if we love ourselves more, then we'll love others better and we'll have more love to give. But the opposite is true. God first loved us so we could share that love with the rest of His children. In the story of the Good Samaritan (Luke 10:25-37), the Levite and the priest loved themselves. The Samaritan loved his neighbor.

God's Word is so powerful that it can also have a ripple effect in our lives. It's your choice whether the ripple will be the lies you're told or the truth of God's Word. Let's quiet the lies or, better yet, silence them all together.

Shout the Praise

I have a friend that I don't get to see very often. But when I do, she always makes me feel like a million bucks. No matter what is going on in her life, she always makes me feel as if I'm the most important person in the room. She is genuinely bummed out when I am, and she rejoices with me in my little successes.

She is everyone's biggest cheerleader. She shouts the praise of others in her life rather than knocking them down to feel better about herself.

We do that, don't we? We knock people down sometimes because we have this warped view that only one of us can succeed. But the truth is God is enough. He can bless both you and me in our pursuits in this life. So, even if she succeeds, it doesn't lessen my chances of success. If she is blessed, it doesn't take away from my blessings.

Recognizing the good in something can change the way we feel about a situation. It's so easy to focus on the bad, the things going wrong. But that only creates more wishes. We know there are good things, and when we choose to focus on those, our attitude changes to gratitude. When we readjust our focus, we recognize that God is still here, mending our cups so they can fill with joy and peace.

Let's take a page from my friend's life and be cheerleaders for one another. Let's find joy and freedom in finding the good and shouting the praise of others.

Serve Others

God has given each of us different gifts. Discover yours and use them to serve Him. 1 Peter 4:10 says, "As each has received a gift, use it to serve one another, as good stewards of God's varied grace." When you are fulfilled and satisfied with what God has given you and where He has placed you, then peace, joy, and contentment are yours. Putting others first and serving them is a fast track to true contentment.

Our primary purpose is to bring glory to God and to point people to Jesus. By serving the people God has placed in our lives, we are ultimately fulfilling our purpose of glorifying God.

Recognize the Seasons

Waiting can be difficult. To be content while waiting takes some spiritual muscle. I have found much encouragement from Psalm 1.

> Blessed is the man who walks not in the counsel of the wicked, nor stands in the way of sinners, nor sits in the seat of scoffers; but his delight is in the law of the LORD, and on his law he meditates day and night. He is like a tree planted by streams of water that yields its fruit in its season, and its leaf does not wither. In all that he does, he prospers.
>
> —Psalm 1:1-3

There are so many nuggets of truth in the first three verses alone. If we walk with the Lord and delight ourselves in His Word rather than live life for ourselves, we will bear fruit.

But sometimes we expect to bear fruit all the time since we're walking with the Lord and serving Him and following His lead in our lives. That's not the case. Not every season is fruit-bearing season. Some seasons are for waiting. Some are for growing. Some are for pruning. And some are for bearing fruit.

I have an avocado tree. Though I wish it produced avocados year-round, it doesn't. Sometimes we compare our lives with someone else who is in the fruit-bearing season when we're not. When we do that, forget having a leaky cup. We might as well turn our cup over and pour out all our joy.

If we recognize the season and remember that seasons change, we have hope. Also keep in mind that God is still at work, regardless of which season it is. Whether it's the chaos season or the perseverance season or the calm before the storm, God is working. And He's more concerned with our character development during each season than the circumstances of the season.

Know that each season will not last forever. Your seasons will change. Your mission fields will change. But I encourage you to keep the big picture in mind. Keep the end goal in your thoughts because then you can be content in any season, knowing your greater purpose is still moving forward.

Where will you find your satisfaction today? Will you focus on your circumstances, or will you trust God? Will you look at those around you and allow jealousy and envy to form, or will you encourage them and be their cheerleader because you are confident in who you are in Christ? Will you continue to make wishes, or will you be content in bringing glory to God? It's time to make the decision to mend your cup and allow the joy to fill you up!

CHAPTER FOUR

Walk Out of the Pit

I was overwhelmed as I sat down to write today. My morning began as always while it was still dark. I had to get myself ready before my four kids woke up. And as the sun rose, so did the chaos. One child yelled from the bathroom because the poop wouldn't come out. Another asked me to sign papers they forgot to have me sign. While signing those papers, another child called for me from his room. He was in tears and needed some calming down. So, we talked and prayed.

I rushed back to the kitchen to finish making breakfast and pack lunches. (Or at least I attempted to pack lunches. I didn't go to the store yesterday, so we were out of almost everything.) Cue the kid telling me he doesn't have any lettuce to give his tortoise because we're out. Then a kid shouted from the bedroom that they can't find underwear. I told them to go search the clean laundry pile. Meanwhile, my husband told me about the medical bill that came in the mail, and it was much higher than I anticipated.

The kitchen had the dirty dishes from breakfast (and dinner, lunch, and breakfast from the day before). The counter was covered in peanut butter and cracker crumbs. The bathroom had toothpaste all over the counter and water all over the floor. I had no idea how or why there was a flood in my bathroom.

I sat and stared at the mess, my mind processing all the emotions and battles our family just fought. I looked at my calendar and the list of things I had to do today. I glanced at my weary eyes in the mirror and thought, *I can't do this!*

Have you ever had one of those days? Maybe not those same circumstances, but have you had a day where you felt everything was coming at you at once or everything was falling apart? I know there are many women out there having days similar to mine. We have too many responsibilities; too many things weigh on our shoulders. Maybe our expectations of how life should be are too high. We want everything to be perfect, but perfect only happened in the Garden of Eden.

The Pit

There's a story I heard long ago about a farmer who discovered that his donkey had fallen into a deep pit. The donkey was in great distress, and the farmer could not figure out a way to rescue the donkey from the hole. Finally, the farmer decided that since the animal was old and the pit needed to be filled in, he would bury the donkey. This would fill the pit and spare the donkey a slow, agonizing death from starvation. He picked up his shovel and began to fill in the hole.

There are so many days like today where I feel like I'm the donkey being buried alive. The needs of my family, the messy house, the to-do list, my job, the emotions (mine and my children's), and the responsibilities are piling up, and I don't know if I'll survive. Sometimes life can be so overwhelming that we simply have no clue what to do or where to go. And if you're at all like me, tears quickly rise to the surface because you don't know how to move forward. The emotions can be paralyzing and exhausting.

It's the Little Things

I'm grateful to have food and clothes for my kids. I'm grateful to have a house for our family. But sometimes it all overwhelms me. I sit and stare at the hundred cups that have accumulated since I last did the dishes, and I feel defeated before I even begin.

It's what we call the "little" things that puncture our cups the most. It's the day-to-day things that can drain our joy almost quicker than the big, scary things that happen to us. Laundry by itself is not a huge deal. Neither are dishes nor packing lunches. Even coaching my child through his anxiety so he can get to school is doable. These individually may pierce a tiny hole that leaks joy, but it's when they are piled on top of each other that my soul can't withstand the pressure, and what began as a tiny pinhole becomes a gaping pothole.

So, how do we stop this pattern? How do we ensure joy in our lives when the little things threaten to take it? Here are a few ideas that have helped me.

One at a Time

Think about one project at a time rather than the whole. Don't try to tackle the entire to-do list in one moment or solve every problem in one day. Take one thing at a time.

When my son started sixth grade, he was overwhelmed when he thought about every class he had. He had to switch to a new room and new teacher six times, and it was too much at first. The best coping mechanism for him was to think only about the class he was currently in. When he thought about the six classes ahead of him, he became anxious. But thinking about one class at a time made the day less overwhelming, and he was able to conquer his fears.

I remember my first year in college. It was finals week, and I had a ten-page paper due in one class and a presentation in another. I had to edit and produce a piece for the school cable show and read a book and write a report on it for another class. I was overwhelmed. My mentor at the time told me to take care of each assignment one at a time. "You can't do them all at once." So, I sat down and wrote out which was due first, which needed the most time and the most attention. I conquered them one at a time and went from feeling paralyzed by the overload to finishing every single project on time.

Write It Out

Sometimes all we need to do is get everything out of our heads and onto paper for a little bit of clarity. This may sound simple, but if your brain is anything like mine, getting thoughts out of your head and onto paper will free up your mind and help you focus on a task with more clarity because you won't have your entire to-do list floating around as well. You'll be able to focus more and be more productive.

I like writing to-do lists for two reasons. It helps me tackle one thing at a time. But it also allows me to see progress. I can check off "clean the table" when I've cleaned it. So, even though two hours later it's messy again, I can look at my list and know I got something accomplished. Sometimes I look around and know I was busy all day but can't figure out what I did. I look at my list, and it reminds me.

Writing it out has also helped me through the overwhelming emotions. When I take time to download not only my to-do list but also my emotions onto paper, I'm able to process through them a little easier. I started doing this in the form of a blog. I rarely posted what I wrote, but I wrote down what I was feeling, what I was struggling with, and what I was learning about God through it all. Once my emotions were out of my head and on paper, they seemed more manageable. I could see them from a different perspective.

Delegate (If You Can)

We can't delegate everything like work projects, but I bet you can find something on your to-do list that you can give to someone else. When I come home and I'm overwhelmed by the pile of laundry, I ask my kids to help. They don't do it perfectly (or even close to perfectly) but having them take care of the laundry frees me up to work on the bigger issues.

Accept Imperfection

My kids don't fold the laundry the way I want, and they certainly don't put the clothes in their drawers as efficiently as I do. But if I want to be less overwhelmed, I must let the little things go. Figure out what details really matter and which ones can be imperfect, and then let them be.

It's also okay for me to be imperfect. I always expect the best of myself, and when the weaknesses shine brighter than the strengths, it can overwhelm me. However, I've learned that the weaknesses are okay. While the Holy Spirit works on transforming me and molding me into the person God desires, God works through my weaknesses to show how big He is and to bless me because I persevered and found joy through the struggle.

Say No

It might be time to take something off your plate or to empty it altogether. I'm a huge advocate for finishing what you've started and delivering on a promise. So, I'm not advocating you quit something in the middle for no reason. However, there are times when walking away from something is necessary. Maybe you've received a new medical diagnosis, and you can't do things as you used to. Or your kids are pulling you in every direction between sports and homework, and you can't keep up. It's completely okay to say "no" or "not right now." There may be a time in the future when "yes" will be your answer. Everything really does come in seasons.

Saying "no" is hard for me because I love everything I'm involved in. When I started writing this book, my responsibilities began to overwhelm me. I already had a lot on my plate at the kids' school, at church, and with the chores at home. Add writing a book and creating a new business to the list, and I was in over my head. So, I started looking at my commitments, and I found a few things that, although I didn't want to give them up, I knew they would be in capable hands. And I don't regret it because I get to watch other women serve the Lord through their gifts, and I get to focus on what the Lord is asking me to do. It's a win-win!

Embrace the Situation

There are sometimes when no matter what we try, we can't get out of our overwhelming circumstances, and we need to embrace the situation for what it is.

My cousin has a little girl, who is such a blessing to their family, but she has had some struggles—really big struggles. She was in the hospital for over five months in her first seven months of life. As I write this, she is back in the hospital. My cousin is feeling the weight of all the ups and downs with her daughter. She longs to take her home. She is torn between the hospital and home where she has three other kids that need their mama. The crazy schedule is wearing on all of them. But she can't take one thing off her plate. She didn't ask for the situation or desire it, but she has learned to accept it and is doing the best she possibly can in the middle of it all.

Count it all joy, my brothers, when you meet trials of various kinds, for you know that the testing of your faith produces steadfastness. And let steadfastness have its full effect, that you may be perfect and complete, lacking in nothing.

—James 1:2-4

I know there are moments when counting our trials *all joy* seems impossible. Yet, God says we have every reason to rejoice because He is working. At the very minimum our perseverance is growing, and we are being molded into perfection, a state in which we will lack nothing. And I delight in this result. But I do not delight in the process.

As a teenager I was a CILT (Camper in Leadership Training). It was a two-year program for developing leadership skills. It was one of the best and hardest things I did in high school. At the graduation ceremony each graduate stood up and shared a symbol that represented their life with God. I chose a piece of silver. It wasn't fancy. It wasn't polished, but it was valuable. Here's why I chose it.

Silver is never pure when found in the earth. It is mixed with other metals or minerals like copper or manganese. Silver must be refined. It is placed in a crucible and heated in a furnace to extreme temperatures (over 1700°F). As the silver melts, all the impurities in the metal rise to the surface and the dross is skimmed off. The silver may be reheated again to see if any more impurities remain. This process continues until no impurities come to the surface and the silversmith can see his reflection perfectly in the crucible.

I absolutely love this image. It reflects the trials and tribulations of this life so well. In Isaiah 48:10 the Lord says, "Behold, I have refined you, but not as silver; I have tried you in the furnace of affliction." This is why perseverance is so important. We have impurities that make us more like the world than Christ. So, into the furnace we go. It may get really hot, and it may get really hard. But the process refines us and makes us into the image we were created to be in the first place. And if we hang in there, if we have perseverance, the outcome will be absolutely worth it. With each trial God looks into our crucible and sees more and more of Himself.

Developing perseverance is hard. It is not easy to be boiled. It hurts, it's uncomfortable, and it's simply not fair. But I cling to the promise that He is refining me and that He is with me. When it feels like I'm in a boiling pot and I say to myself, *I don't think I can do this any longer*, a verse comes to mind that reminds me that I *can* do this because God is with me and working in me to make something amazing, something beautiful and even more valuable.

During this overwhelming season of your life, it may feel like you are burning in the fire with no way out. My cousin felt as if she was at a constant boil with no cooling point. I say this to her, to you, and myself—hang in there. Find courage in knowing the situation will shape you into the woman God designed you to be. And remember that God is with you the entire way.

Understand You're Not Alone

This overwhelming season becomes dangerous if we isolate ourselves, allowing loneliness to surround us. We may not do it on purpose. In the crazy season of raising four kids aged five and under, I couldn't get out of the house. By the time I got all four dressed and ready, it was time for the youngest ones to take a nap. I felt overwhelmed and lonely.

But you know what? God met me in my loneliness. He saw me when no one else did. He comforted me when there was no one else to comfort me. I learned I could rely on Jesus for support during this time. I had always been taught to turn to Jesus, who would comfort me, but I found a new depth to this statement during this time of immense loneliness. I dug deep into the Scriptures as much as I could and learned and grew, and my loneliness began to disappear. I was comforted by Jesus and His Words. His joy filled me up.

You may not be struggling through raising babies and toddlers. You may be working in a cubicle surrounded by people that you don't exactly see eye-to-eye with, and you feel isolated and alone. I have found that sometimes it's when we're surrounded by tons of people that we can feel the loneliest.

Hang in there. God may be doing something incredible in your life. Paul says that we are a new creation when we trust Jesus as our Savior (2 Corinthians 5:17). But that new creation requires transformation, which takes time. The Bible calls this *sanctification*. The chaos, loneliness, and trials might be part of how He is bringing you into a new creation. And God will use the dirt that is piled up on top of us for our ultimate deliverance.

I never finished the story about the donkey. You know what happened? The donkey didn't die. With each shovel of dirt the owner threw into the pit, the donkey shook it off its back and stepped on top. Eventually, the hole filled with dirt, and the donkey stood atop the soil, able to walk out of the pit.

God wants to relieve you from being overwhelmed. He wants to remove you from your isolation. He longs to fill your pit with dirt so you can walk out. Just remember that even while the pit is filling up, you are not alone. Jesus is with you, and He's the best companion.

Fear not, for I have redeemed you; I have called you by name, you are mine. When you pass through the waters, I will be with you; and through the rivers, they shall not overwhelm you; when you walk through fire you shall not be burned, and the flame shall not consume you. For I am the LORD your God, the Holy One of Israel, your Savior.

—Isaiah 43:1b-3a

Read God's Word and Pray

Peter, Jesus's disciple, wanted to walk out to Jesus on the water (Matthew 14). But when he stepped out of the boat and took his eyes off Jesus, he quickly found himself afraid and sinking beneath the waves. He called out to Jesus for help. We are no different than Peter. When we are stressed and reach our breaking point, we must communicate with Jesus to feel His comfort and receive His peace.

Reading the Scriptures is how we communicate. He talks to us through His Word, and we respond in prayer and through our actions. The number one most important step you can take towards overcoming the pit is reading God's Word.

There is a peace and calm that comes when reading Scripture. As you read His Word, respond with prayer. Ask God for His strength when you are most weary. Ask Him for discernment with what job to do next and wisdom in disciplining your kids. Ask Him to give you His outlook so you will be overwhelmed by His presence instead of your responsibilities. He can take anything you give Him and will hear every word you pray (1 Peter 3:12).

It is okay to be broken. But we must realize that no matter how much we try to fix our brokenness on our own, we can't help ourselves. We must embrace God's strength and wisdom, acknowledging that we need God and that He alone can mend us. Then we must allow Him to do just that.

Find Community

During a season of loneliness when my kids were little, I was invited to join a women's Bible study. It included childcare, so I could go with all my kiddos. I went in thirsty and craving companionship. I didn't realize how much I truly needed it until I got it, and my soul began to fill up. God used those ladies in my life to bring my joy back. They taught me many things, and it was through one of the Bible studies that my own transformation began.

As I began to share more of my story with others and open up about life's journey and struggles, others opened up about their struggles too. I found a whole new community. I was not alone—far from it. I was now part of a bigger picture.

God made us to be in relationship. That truth is found in the beginning of Genesis. "It is not good that the man should be alone" (Genesis 2:18). That verse references marriage and a man-and-woman relationship. But the truths of relationship apply across the board. God created us to be in fellowship, in relationship and community. We need each other.

God has used people in my cousin's life to help ease her overwhelming situation. Her mother has been able to help with the kiddos at home. The nurses have taken amazing care of her daughter in the NICU when she can't be there. She has friends and family all over the country lifting her up in prayer and providing her with encouragement and support. God uses people in very powerful ways to heal us and to provide for our needs.

If you don't have other believers encouraging you and uplifting you, joy will remain elusive. You can't do this alone. I am grateful to live in an age where we have technology that can bring us together even when we can't come together physically. Getting together face-to-face is incredible and uplifting and necessary. However, if you find yourself in a situation that requires you to stay home, you must do whatever you can to still connect with other believers. Your joy depends on it!

If I'm honest, sometimes being with other believers can steal my joy. Sometimes personal conflicts try to override my determination to have joy. But I can't ignore Paul's teaching in Philippians about partnership in the gospel and how it sustains his joy. Paul's joy came from the people in his life. Paul rarely thanked God for things. Instead he constantly thanked God for people. And those people remained a source of joy. Although true contentment comes from God and His Word, joy is amplified because of the people He places in our lives.

Just remember—relationships are imperfect. If we expect them to be perfect, then we will be disappointed and end up in isolation again. Loneliness will settle in. I've learned that perfection is not where joy lies. It's in the imperfections. It's in the adventure of our everyday.

Friends won't bring you contentment. Only Jesus can do that. But He has designed us to be in community, and we will flourish in our relationship with Him when we are intimately connected to others who know Him.

The Lord Will Provide

A.W. Tozer once said, "Sometimes when we get overwhelmed, we forget how big God is."[11] I remember being newly pregnant with our second child. I was still in the morning sickness phase, and Tim was laid off from his job. It was the height of the housing market crash and he worked for a mortgage company. Because we knew the lay-off was inevitable, Tim had already begun looking for a new job. He was only out of work for a few weeks. We were so thankful to the Lord for providing for us, especially since we had our own home to pay for, a one-year-old at home, and another baby on the way.

Tim didn't like his new job, but he faithfully went without complaint because he knew so many of his coworkers were still out of work and finding another job would be difficult. Three months flew by, and Tim had his ninety-day review with his boss at his new job. Tim called me right after the meeting. I was expecting good news, hoping for a raise. Instead, I heard, "They let me go. I'm coming home."

We were now without any income. We looked at the mounting bills, including our mortgage. We considered selling our home because we couldn't afford the payments, but because of the housing market crash, we were completely upside down and owed more than the house was worth. And we still had student loan payments. On top of that, our family was growing, and all the expenses of two little boys were looming over us. We looked at our responsibilities, and we were overwhelmed. It felt like we were in the pit and the walls were caving in.

We needed to remember that our God is big and that He created everything. He cares about the little details, and we needed to trust Him with the details of our lives. It is so easy for us to put God in a box. But He is sovereign, and He sees the big picture when we can't. He's working behind the scenes, not to make our lives better but to make us more like Him so we may glorify Him.

We don't believe He "caused" all the things to happen to us in that hard season of layoffs. We do believe Him when He says, "I will never leave you, nor forsake you." He was with us even though our pit was filling with dirt.

Sometimes the Lord pulls us out of our pit when we first ask. At other times He fills the hole with dirt so we can climb out. Tim eventually got a new job with an amazing boss and wonderful coworkers. It even came with an insurance change that reduced our medical bills significantly. Not only did our pit fill up so we could walk out, it actually became a mound. It lifted us higher and we were better off than before the pit formed.

Have courage, friend. Find hope today! Feeling overwhelmed, isolated, and lonely is a hard place to be stuck. But there is hope. Take action and follow the suggested steps to remove the overwhelming elements. Dive into God's Word and work on your relationship with Jesus. Reach out to other believers and study His Word together. And ultimately trust that God sees you and does not want to leave you in the pit.

Look around yourself and find the ways that God is filling your pit and rescuing you. It may take time, and it may be in the most unconventional way, but I promise He's working on it.

The best part is that as the Lord redeems us from the things and situations that overwhelm us, from the pits of isolation and loneliness, He puts a new song in our mouths.

[God] drew me up from the pit of destruction, out of the miry bog, and set my feet upon a rock, making my steps secure. He put a new song in my mouth, a song of praise to our God. Many will see and fear and put their trust in the LORD.

— Psalm 40:2-3

As the pit is filling up with dirt, our souls are filling up with joy. What a promise!

CHAPTER FIVE

I'm Not the Pilot

Anxiety is a big issue to tackle in a book. Part of me doesn't even want to try because I fear I'll be misunderstood. But it's important in the conversation of joy. So, here I go.

Anxiety Disorders

I first want to briefly talk about anxiety disorders, including general anxiety disorder, panic disorders, and social anxiety disorders. This in no way is an exhaustive conversation. It merely touches the surface.

General anxiety disorder is an excessive, uncontrollable worry that interferes with daily functioning. Panic disorder describes a person who is overcome by sudden periods of severe fear and even terror. Social anxiety disorder results when everyday interactions with others induce significant anxiety or fear.[12]

The symptoms of these disorders can come on suddenly and unprovoked, or they may be triggered by something or someone. They can last for a moment or for a prolonged period of time. It may seem irrational to everyone else. It's not something that a person can snap out of or overcome with a simple thought.

Anxiety disorders are connected to a chemical or hormonal imbalance. In some cases, the imbalance causes the anxiety. While in other instances, prolonged, uncontrolled anxiety may produce a chemical imbalance. For example, having too much adrenaline for a prolonged period (a panic attack) can alter how your body copes with excess adrenaline in the future. For some, a vitamin or mineral deficiency may be the culprit. These disorders can be remedied by medication, therapy, and diet change.

We as believers in Jesus need to talk about anxiety more and develop compassion for those experiencing it. Anxiety disorders do not develop because a person doesn't have enough faith in God. Let me say that again. Anxiety disorders are not caused by a person's lack of faith in God.

Ask any woman who has experienced menopause about her symptoms. Hot flashes are brutal, and the irritability that accompanies them is next-level. I had surgery in my thirties that sent me into early menopause, so I have experience with this firsthand. I can be okay one moment and crazily irritable the next. Whether it is ticking sounds or heat or simply someone talking, my mind goes crazy, and I can't handle it. It feels like my head will explode, and if I don't escape from whatever is causing the irritability, I will lose control.

No one believes women going through menopause are having hot flashes or irritability because they don't have enough faith in God. That would be silly to think. We know they're experiencing hot flashes and irritability (and even anxiety) because of the hormonal changes happening in their body.

So, why do we say someone suffering with an anxiety disorder due to a chemical imbalance needs to pray more or trust God more? It doesn't work that way.

I do, however, believe God is supreme and can give us peace and joy in the middle of it all. One of the girls in our youth group has been diagnosed with an anxiety disorder. She's heading to college soon, and she was asked if she's nervous about living in a new environment full of strangers. She responded, "I'm still nervous, but I know I'll be okay because God is there."

She then quoted a verse from Philippians. "'Don't be anxious but in everything pray.' I trust that God will give me peace. He'll take care of me even in my anxiety."

She understands that her anxiety does not represent a lack of faith in God. She also knows her faith in God does not mean she'll be anxiety-free, but it lessens the impact. She knows the joy of the Lord will help her through it. She still struggles. God doesn't take her anxiety away, but His joy allows her to know she is going to be okay. She said, "The extra weight and stress of the situation is not on me. I know I'm not doing it alone."

Her faith is not measured by her anxiety. But because her faith is strong, she knows she has a support system that will be with her every step of the way.

If you have an anxiety disorder and you've been told it's all in your head, that you only need to believe in God more or pray harder, I'm here to encourage you. You can get through this. Seek out someone who can help you. Maybe that's a trusted friend or a therapist. You may even need a psychiatrist, who can prescribe medication, or a naturopath doctor, who can check for mineral or vitamin deficiencies and overall gut health.

Thankfully, more people are aware, and more experts are talking about this, which means more resources are available. Ask God to give you discernment and to guide you to the right person or place for help. Remember God loves you and desires to walk with you on this journey.

Worry

With that said, let's talk about anxiety and worry that is not linked to a chemical imbalance. This is likely the worry Paul and Jesus talk about in the Scriptures. If every case of anxiety were unrelated to faith, then Jesus and Paul would have had no reason to discuss the topic. There are worries and times of anxiety that have everything to do with our understanding of Jesus and nothing to do with a chemical imbalance. These moments can overwhelm us and keep us from experiencing true joy. We're going to talk about those worries for the remainder of this chapter.

The word *anxious* translates to *merimnao* in Greek. It means "to be troubled with cares" and "to seek to promote one's interests."[13] I find that definition fascinating. At the onset of a worry, we have the tendency to tell ourselves it's okay. We give ourselves room to worry and call it concern. After all, we would be bad parents if we weren't concerned about our kids. Or we would be a bad friend if we weren't concerned about our friend. But if we really look at the motivation behind our "concern," most often it arises because we either lack control, desire control, or both.

It's the same word Jesus uses when He says in Matthew 6:25, "Do not be anxious about your life, what you will eat or what you will drink, nor about your body, what you will put on. Is not life more than food, and the body more than clothing?" Jesus says He understands the worries of life, but He's got us covered. He takes care of the birds and the flowers. He'll take care of us too.

We may know this verse, yet we say to ourselves, "It's so hard. I try to give it to God, but it's impossible. I'm just a worrier."

A few years ago on the first day of Bible study, the group leader asked us to go around the room and share our name and one word that best describes ourselves. Out of the eighteen women at the table, eight of them chose "worrier." So many women quickly joined in and said, "Oh yeah. I'm a worrier too." Why? Why do we worry? You want to hear the truth? Ladies, we worry because we desire control over the situation, and we don't fully trust God. We don't trust that He means it when He says He cares more about us than a little bird. We don't trust that He'll actually take care of us. I realize that may be rough to hear, but think about it. At the surface we say, "I trust You, Lord," with every intention to leave it in His hands. But we still think about the situation and try to control it.

Keith Minier is the lead pastor at Grace Fellowship in Pickerington, Ohio. At Momentum Youth Conference in 2017, he said, "Why is it that I trust Jesus with my death but not with my life? Why is it that I seek Jesus to save me, but then I don't let Jesus lead me?"[14]

If we are followers of Jesus, we must trust Him with everything. We must trust Him with our plans. We must trust Him with our kids. We must trust Him with our health. We must trust Him in every area.

Trust Fall

I'm sure you've heard of the "trust fall" exercise. In this exercise a blindfolded person must fall backward and trust the person behind them to catch them. We say, "That's easy. I could do that." But so many people get scared as they lean backwards, and instead of falling into the person's arms, they take a step back. They say they trust the person, but truthfully they don't.

I think about the people in my life I truly trust, and the one thing they all have in common is time. I've spent time with each person, and I know personal details about each one. We've laughed together, we've cried together, and we've talked about struggles and hardships together. I know them, and they know me. These are the people I trust.

We say we trust God, but when we must trust Him to catch us when we fall, we fail. We take a step on our own without allowing Him to do the moving for us. And in those moments when I'm struggling with trust, I ask these questions. Do I know Him? Do I spend time with Him? Do I cry and laugh with Him? Do I trust Him?

> Trust in the LORD with all your heart, and do not lean on your own understanding. In all your ways acknowledge him, and he will make straight your paths. Be not wise in your own eyes; fear the LORD and turn away from evil.
>
> —Proverbs 3:5-7

The Hebrew word for *heart* in this verse is *leb*, which translates to "mind or will."[15] We're supposed to trust God with our mind and will and not lean on our own understanding. Yet, so many times we allow our emotions to lead us. We rely on our emotions to guide us.

I can't count how many times my own understanding and my own eyes failed me and led me astray. There are too many.

When we don't "feel" the Lord is near or has our best interest at heart—when we feel we know a better way—we turn to our emotions to guide us. But this verse says we need to *trust in the Lord.*

Trust is hard, especially when we're staring at a situation we don't like. But the truth is that in the moments we don't trust God, we're saying we can do it better and that we want to control the situation.

When I travel via airplane, if it hits turbulence and I get scared and anxious, I don't go to the pilot and tell him I'll fly the plane instead. Of course not. I've never taken any classes on how to fly a plane. The pilot is the one who has the skills and knows what to do if an emergency arises, not me.

God is the Creator of the universe, yet when I get scared, I don't trust Him. I want to control the situation instead of letting Him handle it. I want to fly the plane.

I think of all the times the Israelites thought they knew best and trusted their emotions and their own understanding in a situation only to land in captivity, worse off than they were before.

God is trustworthy. We can trust Him, even in the hard moments when horrible things happen. The sin of man is what caused this world to be broken and frail. It is man who continually turns his back on God, not the other way around.

Yet we sometimes treat God as though He's turned His back on us when bad things happen. We worry that He won't take care of us like we would. We worry He'll abandon us. But if we look into the Scriptures, we see that God never abandoned the Israelites, and He promises to never abandon us either. Throughout the Old and New Testaments, God says over thirty times "I am with you," "I will never leave you," and "I will not forsake you."

Trust is hard, but it's a worthy pursuit!

So, what's a mom (or any person, really) to do? How do we surrender control? Here are a few steps to kick worry to the curb and replace it with trust instead.

Recognize Fear and Replace It with Truth

To say I don't worry about my kids would be a lie. When my oldest started middle school, worries flooded my thoughts. *What friends is he hanging out with? What do they talk about? What kind of language do they use? Are they showing my kid porn? Or is he sitting all alone at lunch because he's not making any friends? What if there is a school shooting?*

I even worry about kids who aren't mine. *My future daughter-in-law is out there somewhere. What is she being exposed to? Is she sexting with boys? Is she making decisions now that will affect her life with my son?* I could go on and on with my worries. The more I let these questions captivate me and consume my thoughts, the more my heartrate quickens, and peace and joy fly right out the window.

Worry is another word for fear. And fear has no place with joy. What is your fear? Say it out loud. Now, what is God's truth? Say it out loud. Do this as many times as necessary!

I do this with my kids all the time. When they have a concern or a fear, we say it out loud. "I'm scared of the spiders." Then, we speak the truth. "They are little, and we are big. They are more scared of us than we are of them. God created them and us, but we are His prized possession. God will protect us."

This eases their minds. It eases mine when I think about the bigger things worrying my brain. Sometimes I wish I was only worried about spiders, but as a mother I have many more fears in life. God's Word says, "perfect love casts out fear" (1 John 4:18). That is truth. God loves me, and I love Him. Because He is with me, I don't need to be afraid.

Pain and suffering are guaranteed in this world. I don't have a choice in that. But I can choose how I will process through the suffering. God says not to worry, so I choose to trust Him! And every time I choose to trust Him instead of freaking out about things I can't control, I find peace.

Pray

Hear me out for a moment. I don't like it when someone says the answer to worry and anxiety is to "pray more" or "pray harder." While there is truth in those statements, there's a lot more involved in truly giving our fears and anxieties over to God. So, when I say we can conquer our anxieties through prayer, I'm not talking a simple prayer of a couple sentences before our meals. I'm talking about a conversation with God, our Creator, who knows exactly what I'm going through and has my days numbered.

> Humble yourselves, therefore, under the mighty hand of God so that at the proper time he may exalt you, casting all your anxieties on him, because he cares for you.
>
> —1 Peter 5:6-7

I've experienced the truth of this verse before. Remember when I sat on the steps outside my house with tears streaming down my face because of my horrible day at school? I sang a song based on these verses. It was a prayer to God, a cry for help. And He answered me. Right there on those steps in a little neighborhood in Buena Park, California, a little freshman girl humbled herself before her Maker and cried out to Him, and God showed up and comforted her.

The most famous verse in the Bible about worry is Philippians 4:6-7. Paul writes, "Do not be anxious (or worry) about anything, but in everything by prayer and supplication with thanksgiving let your requests be made known to God. And the peace of God, which surpasses all understanding, will guard your hearts and your minds in Christ Jesus."

These verses are packed with amazing truths. They promise us peace if we let God know our requests. Instead of worrying about a situation, we have the option to give our requests to God by way of supplication. Supplication means to ask earnestly for something. We're not talking about a shallow, routine prayer. Supplication requires a deep, intimate conversation with our Creator. It's important to be specific and honest with your requests.

I have a fear of buses. I know, you may think that's silly. But the faster the bus goes, the more it shakes and sways, the more I feel like the bus could tip over. My heart rate quickens, and I start imagining worst-case scenarios. Before I know it, I'm overcome by anxiety and panic.

I could pray, *God, please take away my anxiety,* and He might. But my anxiety is caused by something. Ladies, we need to discover the root of our anxiety and ask God to help us with that fear. The more specific we are, the better.

So, instead I pray, *God, I am anxious because I am scared that the bus will tip over, that I will die, and then my kids will be left without a mom. Fear is beginning to control me. My breathing is shallow, and my heart is racing. My thoughts are not based in truth. Please help me, Lord! Remind me of Your truths right now. Slow my breathing. Help me focus on You rather than my fear. Guard my heart and mind as You promised in Philippians because they are freaking out. And grant me Your peace right now. Thank You, Lord.*

Then, I sit and rest in Him. I allow Him to work as I focus on the truths of Scripture that the Holy Spirit brings to mind. I've prayed like this often and not only with buses. I get anxious before speaking, so I utter a similar prayer, stating my fear of man's disapproval. I pray this when I begin to worry about the friends my kids are making at school. I've even prayed this while writing this book. Fear that people won't like me or won't approve of me consumes me all the time. So, I pray and rest in Him. And every time peace comes. It will for you too.

Philippians 4:6-7 doesn't only say "pray." It says, "Pray *with* thanksgiving" (emphasis mine). So, when I find that worry and anxiety fill my thoughts, I change my focus. I think instead about all the things right in front of me I am grateful for. I don't contemplate all the things of the world. I can't handle that in the moment of worry.

I simply look around and thank God for what I see. I thank God for the people with me. I thank God for the adventure I am on. I thank God for the opportunity to do whatever I'm doing. I keep thanking Him for everything He brings to mind. And before I know it, my heart rate slows. My anxiety diminishes little by little until it's nearly gone, sometimes completely gone.

Remember That God Is Bigger

There's a *Veggie Tales* song called "God Is Bigger Than the Boogie Man."[16] I often sang this song to my kids when they were scared at night. It teaches that God is bigger than anything they will come across in life. During those restless nights it spoke truths into their hearts and gave them peace so they could fall asleep.

While we may no longer struggle with the boogie man or monsters under our beds, this truth still applies to our adult-sized fears. He's bigger than any worry or concern plaguing our thoughts. He created the world. Think about that. If He created everything about us and everything around us, then surely He's big enough to help us with our worries.

When we turn to the One who is bigger than us and recognize fear as an opportunity to depend on Him, the fears of life are dwarfed by our big God. We relinquish control to Him, and He grants us courage and gives us strength and power in the Holy Spirit. Our God is bigger and able to do far more than we can ask or imagine (Ephesians 3:20).

As I write this, there was another shooting in Texas at a Walmart during the busy rush of back-to-school shopping. I found myself saying, "God, I trust you. It's those people I don't trust," as I pointed to the picture of the shooter on my computer screen.

I realized that through those words I was allowing fear to return to my thoughts and alter my peace. Worry crept into my mind. Are we safe? Are my kids safe? I took a moment to recognize the fear. I spoke it aloud. And then I said to myself, "Not today. Fear will not be the winner today. My God is bigger. My God is sovereign. My God will take care of me. And even if He doesn't take care of me in the way I prefer, He is still God. He is still good."

Dwell in His Peace

Dwell in His peace, friend! He promises His peace surpasses understanding and guards our hearts and minds in Christ Jesus (Philippians 4:7). This is the best promise ever—it fills my soul with joy more than anything else in the world.

This is the peace that Shadrach, Meshach, and Abednego felt stepping into that furnace. Do you remember the story? Three men faced with the decision to bow down to a statue of the king or honor God chose to trust God even though they faced death in a fiery furnace because of their defiance. They said, "Our God will save us. But if He doesn't, that's okay. We still won't worship the king" (my paraphrase of Daniel 3:17-28). I believe the only way they could have walked into that furnace was through trust in God, knowing they had His peace.

It's a peace that doesn't make sense. I can't even explain it with words. When we watch the news and see school shootings or helicopter crashes or beheadings of believers in other countries, we should be flipping out and panicking and worrying, completely overwhelmed by it all. Yet we can have peace when we trust God and realize He is in control, not us.

And the best part? He gave us the Holy Spirit to help us every step of the way. Before ascending into heaven, Jesus told His followers He would send a helper, the Holy Spirit, to be with us and help us in this life. He then said, "Peace I leave with you; my peace I give to you. Not as the world gives do I give to you. Let not your hearts be troubled, neither let them be afraid" (John 14:27).

Ask for Help

I have trouble with my thyroid. My body has symptoms when I experience a flare. My fingers swell. My hands begin to tremor. My resting heart rate increases. I get exceptionally tired. (This one is hard to distinguish because exhaustion is a chronic condition of motherhood.) My joints ache a lot. Everything hurts. When I experience these symptoms, my body is telling me something is awry.

Our emotions are like symptoms of the heart. If I ignored the symptoms of my thyroid, I could end up in a thyroid storm and possibly die. If we ignore our emotions, we're denying that something is askew in our souls. Sometimes we self-diagnose and self-medicate, which can cause many other problems. We need to get advice from the experts. God created us and is the ultimate expert. So, His Word must be included in our search for answers.

Seeking a counselor who understands emotions and anxiety with a biblical worldview can also be beneficial. You do not need to find the answers on your own. There are many amazing counselors who have studied anxiety and understand the complexity of our human heart and soul. If necessary, seek out a counselor who can guide you as they are guided by the Holy Spirit to bring you into peace and joy.

Let's be women who trust Jesus fully and live an abundant life of peace. Let us live free from worry because we have prayed with thanksgiving, trusted God and His Word, and replaced our fears with truth. Let's not be defined as "worriers" but instead by joy!

CHAPTER SIX

A spoonful of sugar

Every day I hear a story that makes me want to cry. Childhood illness and death, hurricanes and fires, shootings and abuse—bad things happen every day. I hear painful stories of betrayal or domestic violence, stories of deep anguish over the desire to have a child or spouse, or the sudden death of a loved one. It makes my heart break, all the pain we go through.

I remember when two of our dear friends walked through a very difficult situation. They were unable to have children, so they decided to adopt. But the process wasn't easy. They waited a long time to be chosen as adoptive parents. When the day finally came, they were overjoyed. They went to the hospital in great anticipation. They had met the birth mother a few times and even attended a few of her appointments. They had prayed for years for this day and for this baby. Now, they sat waiting to finally take their baby girl home. But they never did. The birth mom changed her mind after the baby was born, and my friends left with an empty car seat. They were devastated.

I know so many of you have stories of loss and sorrow. Most of us have experienced loss in some way, some more than others. I've sat with many friends as they've grieved miscarriages. I remember when a dear friend received her diagnosis of multiple sclerosis and the tears we cried together as she realized her new reality. I've sobbed with dormmates as we grieved the death of a beloved friend. I've prayed over friends as they were faced with the unthinkable task of burying their child.

Sometimes sorrow waits just at the surface, and we can still function and carry on with our lives. Other times, though, sorrow is embedded so deeply we can hardly breathe. We can't move. It feels like we're suffocating.

When someone has been taken from us, it's hard to make sense of it. Well-meaning people say, "All things work together for good," or "They're in a better place," or "At least they're not in pain anymore." But none of that helps the sorrow to disappear. In fact, it can make it worse.

Many times, we are left wondering how a God of love could allow or cause such a tragedy that leads to such sorrow. Even Jesus's own disciples didn't understand why He allowed His friend Lazarus to die, putting his sisters through such grief.

Have you been there? I don't know what you've been through or the details of your sorrow, but I do know that when we are in the middle of grief, God can feel so distant. I know the feeling, and I understand the questions, "Where was God when...?"

Lazarus's sisters posed a similar question. They stated, "Lord, if you had been here, [our] brother would not have died" (John 11:21, 32). Essentially, they were asking, "Where were you, God? Why weren't you here?" Jesus was not with the sisters in their hour of need for a purpose. He did not heal

Lazarus while he was alive for a reason. It didn't make sense to the sisters, and it doesn't always make sense to us either. Raising Lazarus from the dead was a show of His power. But you know what it also shows us? We see His grief. John 11:35 says, "Jesus wept."

Growing up in the church, we joked about this verse because it's the shortest verse in the Bible (depending on what version you read), so when we were asked to quote a verse by memory in class, someone always chose this one.

I soon realized this verse is one of the most important verses in the Bible. Of course, every verse is important, but for me this one made Jesus real. This verse made Jesus click for me. He was God. He was perfect. Even though He was tempted, He was without sin. But when His friend died, he cried. He had emotions like everyone else. He wasn't a robot without feelings. Jesus wept. He was deeply grieved.

A Spoonful of Joy

Sorrow can stop us in our tracks. When it strikes, we don't know how to move forward. I think of my kids when they need to take medicine. They sit there staring at it, belaboring the task of drinking ten milliliters of an unpleasant liquid even though they know it will benefit them.

Medicine sure can taste disgusting. In the musical, *Mary Poppins*, Ms. Poppins provides a solution. "Just a spoonful of sugar helps the medicine go down in the most delightful way."[17] It's no wonder why so many adults prefer a gummy vitamin over a huge multi-vitamin pill. It's filled with sugar. Might I suggest taking a page from Ms. Poppins's book and adding a spoonful of joy to your sorrow?

Have you ever sat down with a friend who has recently lost someone dear to them? Or maybe you have lost someone dear, and someone else comforted you? And through the tears and sadness, someone shares a funny story in remembrance. Laughter erupts and transforms the silence for a moment. Joy and tears together are beautiful. The best part of memorial services for me is having the space to grieve while sharing stories about the person we lost and recognizing how much they impacted our lives.

At the memorial service of my high school mentor, we shared stories of how she poured herself into us. So many stories had people laughing, and it was the best way for us to heal from our loss. It was beautiful. It brought a spoonful of joy into our deep sorrow.

In John 15:11 Jesus says, "These things I have spoken to you, that my joy may be in you, and that your joy may be full." We know Jesus came to give us His joy. Yet He spoke these words within forty-eight hours of His death as He left his best friends and family behind. Could Jesus have felt joy and anticipation for the reunion with His Father and still experienced deep anguish, knowing He would leave His friends and die a horrible death?

As a mother I think of what God must have felt watching His Son tortured and killed. I can't imagine the sorrow, yet there must have been great joy knowing His Son's death and resurrection would make it possible to be reunited with us, something He had been working towards since Eve first sinned in the garden.

The truth is joy is felt most intimately when accompanied by sorrow. The trials we go through, the impossible circumstances we find ourselves in, make joy sweeter. Think of a long, cold winter. It has been cold for what feels like forever. Then, one day the clouds break, and the sun comes out. The air is still cold and crisp all around you, but the sun's rays bring warmth. This is one of my favorite things about springtime. There is nothing better than feeling the sun warm my skin while the cold air swirls around me.

Jesus's joy can have the same effect in a time of sorrow. When I'm in the midst of deep anguish, there is nothing better than feeling Jesus's joy fill me up and warm me from the inside. We can easily be overcome by disappointment and despair. We get stuck. We feel defeated. The sorrow we feel is like an ever-present storm cloud. Yet, with joy we can feel the warmth of the sun.

Here are some actions you can take to help the sun burst through the clouds of your sorrow.

Turn to Jesus

King Hezekiah was deathly ill. God told him through Isaiah to get his affairs in order because his time was nearly done. But Hezekiah cried out to the Lord. He asked God to remember his faithfulness and his wholehearted service to God. The following is God's response.

> I have heard your prayer; I have seen your tears. Behold, I will add fifteen years to your life. I will deliver you and this city out of the hand of the king of Assyria, and will defend this city.
> —Isaiah 38:5b-6

How cool is that? God heard King Hezekiah, and He saw his tears. Psalm 56 says that God keeps track of our tears and puts them in a bottle. The God who created me cares about me and my sorrow.

My friend, cry to Jesus today. He sees you. He hears you. He longs to comfort you. He will sit with you as long as you need. He won't tell you to wipe your tears and move on with your life (until it's time to do so). He won't say the awkward things like "it was meant to be" or "snap out of it." He says instead, "I've got you, and I've got this situation. I won't let go, and I am working. I'll carry you through."

He died for you. He went to the ends of the earth to be with you for eternity. There is joy in knowing that Jesus wins and we are heirs to His throne. That's why John (Jan) Hus, a pre-Reformation martyr, sang and recited Psalms as they lit the wood below him before he burned to death in 1415. Even in that moment he found joy in Jesus. So many others like him willingly gave their lives while still possessing joy because they knew Jesus. They loved Jesus.

Now, I realize that those are extremes, and it's rarely black-and-white. And while it's definitely not easy, it is possible. Be consumed with Jesus instead of your sorrow or circumstances. That perspective will mend any holes allowing the joy to seep out, and before you know it, your cup will be overflowing again.

The apostle Paul knew about suffering and sorrow. He was stoned and imprisoned. He was shipwrecked three times. He was beaten, whipped, and left for dead several times (2 Corinthians 11). Yet, he was filled with joy. He understood that joy comes from Jesus, from seeing fellow believers live for Jesus, and by telling others about Jesus. He said, "For me to live is Christ and to die is gain" (Philippians 1:21). The only reason he had to live was Christ. The joy he found while chained in prison was Christ Himself and seeing others come to know Christ.

Do you need a reason to rejoice today? Have you lost the perspective of joy because of your sorrow? If you believe in Jesus as Savior and Messiah, then you have the best reason ever to rejoice regardless of what situation or difficulty or loss you find yourself in. You know the reason for rejoicing is because Jesus conquered the grave. Keep your eyes on Him. He will always be the source of joy and the reason to possess it.

Let Others Help You

One of the best things you can do is let others help you. This can happen in several ways. If they offer to bring a meal, let them. They wouldn't be offering if they didn't want to help. If they send a card of encouragement, let their words fill your heart. If they offer to pick up your kids, let them. Don't feel that you need to do it all. Don't feel that you are burdening anyone, especially if they offer. There will come a season when you can help others. This may be your season to accept their love and support.

Think back to a time when you saw a friend in a hard season. Maybe they were suffering with loss or felt they were drowning with responsibilities. Think of the things you desired to do for them and how it made you feel when they let you do them or perhaps how you felt when they turned you down. Remember, letting others help us is a way of allowing God to work. All of us want to feel needed and useful. Let others help you.

Don't Let Sorrow Linger

Sometimes we allow sorrow to overstay its welcome. We absolutely need time to grieve the immediate loss, and grief will never go away completely. But there is a fine line before sorrow becomes part of our identity and we are consumed.

Allowing sorrow to consume us robs us of the joy brought into our lives by the person we're mourning. We need to live by honoring their memory without being overwhelmed by the sorrow.

Some of you have been overcome by sorrow for more than weeks or months. It's been years. You don't only feel the sorrow during the holidays or special events. You feel it every single day as deeply as the first day.

Though joy and sorrow can coexist, if sorrow lingers and you dwell in the sorrow, the grief can become all kinds of things that will rob you of joy. It can become bitterness. It can become self-pity. It can even become an obsession. Grief can become a wall we hide behind because we fear even more hurt. It doesn't make much logical sense, but we allow ourselves or even force ourselves to remain within grief. After all, if we're already there, then we can't experience grief again.

We have a choice. We can either live with loss and sorrow and let it motivate us to love others, or we can let it control us, consume us, and hold us down in a pit where we begin to bury ourselves. Don't let this be you.

Remember your loved ones. Remember them in special ways during special events. Do something in their honor that will bring you joy. And let the tears fall. But allow joy to mingle with the sorrow and allow the Lord's hope to light your soul.

Focus on Others

One of the best ways to mix sorrow and joy is to focus on others. I saw this firsthand with a dear friend of mine. Her grandmother passed away, and instead of sitting at home with her grief, she decided to spend time volunteering at the assisted-living home where her grandmother had lived. Some of her friends, myself included, wondered if it would increase her sorrow, but it did the opposite. It allowed her to grieve the loss of her grandmother and find joy in the company of many of her friends.

Praying for others and sharing your story with others can have a great impact on your joy and sorrow. In the same way that sitting with someone who has already been there will help you, you can be that encouragement for someone else. Turn your story into a testimony of how God has walked you through the sorrow. Even if you're still struggling, sharing your story and making yourself vulnerable will encourage others on their journeys.

Ask God to guide you to a place where you can focus on others. He will meet you in this place and provide comfort and joy in the most unexpected ways.

Get Professional Help (If Necessary)

There's a sorrow that takes you deeper than grief. It takes you to a place where you can't get out of bed. You don't feel the desire to do anything. You've tried relying on Jesus, and you desire with all your being to do so, but you still feel like nothing matters anymore. It may be depression.

Sorrow should never lead you to desperation because Jesus is there to help you through. Grief will feel overwhelming at times, but not so much that you want to end your life. If you find yourself at the end of your rope and feeling like this life isn't worth it, seek Jesus but also pursue professional help. We need to be aware of the mind, body, and spirit. You must seek treatment just as you would if you had a brain tumor. Clinical depression is a serious issue. Don't go through it alone. Find a good biblical therapist who can help you as you turn to Jesus.

Beyond Your Own Sorrow

For those of us desiring to walk alongside a friend who is in a season of sorrow, here's a tip on what to say and what not to say.

Don't ask, "Are you okay?" Because honestly, they probably aren't, but they are managing the best they can. And some moments they might be okay, and some moments they feel like their world is caving in. Even years later, especially on anniversaries, the question "Are you okay?" can be impossible to answer.

Instead ask, "How are you handling things today?" This gives them the freedom to share how they are in that moment. Maybe they're on an upswing of the emotional rollercoaster. Maybe they're overwhelmed by the process. This question gives them space to answer honestly.

Then, sit and listen. Make yourself comfortable with the silence, with the sorrow in the room. You don't have to solve anything. You don't have to fix anything. You can't. So just be with them. And in the process you will bring them joy and be filled with joy yourself.

It Is Well

Have you heard the story behind the hymn "It Is Well"? Horatio Spafford lost his son at age two. Shortly after that the Chicago fires devastated him financially because of his property investments throughout the city. He had plans to go back to England with his family for a time, but because of important meetings he stayed in Chicago while his family went on ahead of him. While at sea, their ship was struck and sunk. Spafford's four daughters perished. Only his wife survived. He quickly traveled to meet up with his wife, and as his boat neared the spot where his daughters died, he penned the now famous hymn, "It Is Well with My Soul."

Spafford's faith in Jesus brought him joy in the middle of great sorrow. To lose five children and all his wealth must have brought him great anguish. Yet he wrote:

When peace like a river, attendeth my way,
When sorrows like sea billows roll;
Whatever my lot, Thou has taught me to know,
It is well, it is well, with my soul.[18]

Most of us probably know the third phrase as "Whatever my lot, Thou has taught me to *say*." I'm guessing the word *know* in the original text was changed to *say* so that it would rhyme with *way*. But I love that the original version says "Thou has taught me to *know*." It's easy to *say* something. However, to *know* something implies intimacy. It is more than mere knowledge. It is a deep belief rooted in experience. When we're intimate with Jesus in the good times, we experience His faithfulness. Then, in the hard times of sorrow, we too can *know* "it is well" because He has proved Himself faithful.

Friend, I too grieve over the losses that are part of the human condition. My heart breaks over the pain experienced by each one of us. I too have wrestled with reaching a place where I can say "It is well with my soul."

There is hope—not only for the future but also for the present moment. The good news is you don't have to trade your sorrow to embrace His joy. My prayer for us both is that we don't delay any longer and embrace His comfort while He fills us with His joy one spoonful at a time.

CHAPTER SEVEN

My Joy Is Not for Sale

I love a good garage sale. I attended one where several books were displayed on a beautiful bookshelf. The bookshelf itself was not for sale, only the books on the shelf. The bookshelf was clearly marked with a bold sign that read: "Bookshelf Not for Sale."

Well, a woman approached the homeowner and asked how much the bookshelf cost. The owner replied, "It's not for sale." The woman proceeded to offer an amount for the shelf. The owner replied again, "It's not for sale." The woman then offered an even larger amount for the bookshelf, adding, "Everyone has their price." The owner, now a bit agitated, said very forcefully, "The bookshelf. Is not. For sale!" The woman rolled her eyes, let out a huff, and went on her way.

There are times when I feel like this homeowner. People and situations vie for my joy like it's for sale, and they'll do anything they can to get it. Sometimes I just want to scream,

"My joy. Is not. For sale!" How about you? Have you ever felt that way?

Bill of Sale

One of my favorite musicals from my childhood is *Pete's Dragon* (1977).[19] Pete is a little boy running away from the Gogan family who bought Pete as a slave. He finds Miss Nora, a kind woman, who takes him and cares for him. One day in the center of town, there is an argument between Miss Nora and the Gogans.

In great musical fashion they burst into song, going back and forth. The Gogans claim they have a bill of sale for Petey. They threaten to bring Nora before the judge if she doesn't hand Pete over. Of course, Nora refuses and even threatens to hurt them if they try. Elliot, the dragon, comes to Pete's defense, and the Gogans's boat gets hit. As they sink into the water, they wave the bill of sale in the air and sing as they sink below the water. It's a fantastic showdown.

Sometimes I feel like my struggle is summed up perfectly in this little song. Even if something or someone shows up claiming to have a bill of sale for our joy, we don't have to hand it over. The team member at my job who causes drama and always makes me out to be the bad guy cannot have my joy. The lady at Target who takes the parking spot I've been patiently waiting for cannot have my joy. My autoimmune disease cannot have my joy. Anger cannot have my joy. My kids cannot have my joy even though they try super hard at bedtime!

I used to think things or people stole my joy. But it's not true. I willingly hand it over all the time.

What does that look like? What does it look like to willingly give joy away? I have countless stories of giving my joy away. Sometimes I have given it away completely, cup and all. Other times, I've only allowed a little joy to leak out.

When someone is rude or unkind to me, I give away my joy like candy. I become sassy or even lash back, and I willingly surrender my joy. I let them "get" to me. I no longer have joy in that moment. It's hard to have joy in the same heart space as anger and hate and pride. This kind of situation arises all the time.

A long time ago I had an altercation with a mother accusing me of being unkind and unfair to her daughter. She cornered me in a public place and began to accuse me, becoming very vocal about her feelings. I handled myself the best I could in that moment. But as soon as I could get out of there, I ran outside, and tears poured down my face. I spent the next couple weeks rehashing the conversation in my mind and second guessing my decision and my actions. I was miserable. I let this situation affect how I handled everything else. I allowed it to alter my joy.

Some Things Are Worth Fighting For

Sometimes we must fight for joy. The world is not all rainbows and unicorns. Some days it feels like I'm in the middle of a war, and I must fight with all the tools at my disposal. I've got to keep my joy safe. And the war isn't always with other people. Sometimes it's with my own body.

In early 2012 I was up in the mountains with my family, and my heart felt like it was going to burst out of my chest. It was beating so fast. I didn't know what was going on, but it didn't feel good. It eventually calmed down, but it happened two more times while I was up there. It continued happening even after we came home. I had no idea at the time, but my thyroid was malfunctioning, and it turns out it had been doing so for a while.

I had chronic fatigue and trouble remembering things. I always figured that was due to pregnancy brain or mere exhaustion. I didn't realize these were symptoms of an auto-immune disease. Some of these symptoms I'd had for over ten years.

I remember during life when I worked full-time outside the home, I would get so desperate for a nap in the middle of the day even though I'd had at least eight hours of sleep. I simply couldn't keep my eyes open. It was so bad that sometimes I fell asleep at my desk. I noticed my hands would shake at times, kind of like my grandpa, who had Parkinson's disease. I also felt a lot of pain in my joints and muscles. There were days when I would wake up in tears from the pain. At one point in my twenties, I was taking Advil and Tylenol every three hours around the clock.

It turns out these were all symptoms of an undiagnosed autoimmune disorder. Once I was diagnosed with Graves' disease in 2012, I was put on medication for my heart and for my thyroid. This helped significantly. And after doing a lot of research on my own, I was able to get almost all my symptoms under control through stringent dietary restrictions. I was doing really well.

But then in 2018 my ovaries were removed, sending me into menopause. Since that surgery, I have been fighting hard. Even with strict eating, it feels like my body is under constant attack and always inflamed. The lack of hormones is a constant struggle. Trying to find the right hormone replacement for my body has been challenging. Some have caused rapid weight gain. Some have made no difference. None have been successful in taking away hot flashes and other not-so-great menopause symptoms.

If I'm honest, there are days when it's a battle to keep my joy. I feel I'm constantly saying, "My joy. Is not. For sale."

Have you ever been there? Have you been in a space where your physical body is not where you'd like it to be, and it's a constant battle to keep a joy-filled soul? Maybe it's not an autoimmune disease. Maybe it's cancer. Maybe it's arthritis or diabetes. Maybe it's another condition that has you on medication that causes bad "side effects." I know the struggle is real for so many of us. We have an idea of what we'd like our life to be like. And when that idea or plan doesn't work out, joy can be elusive.

So, what can we do differently? How do we stop handing our joy over to others? How do we keep circumstances and difficulties from draining our cup?

Get Ready to Fight

It feels like we're in a war because we are. Paul says that we are in a battle and that it's "not against flesh and blood" but takes place in the spiritual world (Ephesians 6). But thankfully, he tells us what we need to do to fight that battle.

Put On the Armor

Finally, be strong in the Lord and in the strength of his might. Put on the whole armor of God, that you may be able to stand against the schemes of the devil. For we do not wrestle against flesh and blood, but against the rulers, against the authorities, against the cosmic powers over this present darkness, against the spiritual forces of evil in the heavenly places. Therefore take up the whole armor of God, that you may be able to withstand in the evil day, and having done all, to stand firm.

—Ephesians 6:10-13

Paul also mentions six pieces of armor, five of which are defensive pieces that protect our hearts, our minds, and our faith. They are the belt of truth, the breastplate of righteousness, the shoes of the gospel of peace, the shield of faith, and the helmet of salvation. These five pieces allow us to shield ourselves from the attacks of the enemy and stand firm in battle.

The last piece of armor is the only offensive weapon. It slays our enemies and our situations. This weapon is the sword of the Spirit. This is the Bible. We can use God's Word to fight our battles. I'm determined not to let my physical body and medical issues drain my cup. I'm determined to not let others steal my joy. So, I fight for it. I don't sit down and accept defeat. I put on my armor. I constantly protect my cup and shield my joy from the enemy's grasp by digging into God's Word every day.

We hear this so often as believers in Christ that we tune it out, removing the weight of it. But reading the Bible is the best weapon in this fight. It's our sword. We can't go to battle without a sword. If we do, we'll lose. Yet we do it all the time as believers in Jesus. We walk out the door without getting ready for battle. Let's stop it right now. Let's plan today to put on our armor every day.

Find Your Worth and Joy in Jesus

We must find our worth and joy in Jesus, not in pleasing others or in their opinions of us. There are so many places in Scripture telling us our worth is found in Christ. There are two chapters I go to first, though. Isaiah 43 and 1 Peter 2.

Here are statements from Isaiah 43 that I speak out loud often.

1. God created me (verse 1).
2. God formed me (verse 1).
3. God redeemed me (verse 1).

4. God calls me by name (verse 1).
5. I am His (verse 1).
6. He will protect me (verse 2).
7. He is my God (verse 3).
8. He has paid my ransom (verse 3).
9. I am precious in His eyes (verse 4).
10. He loves me (verse 4).
11. He is with me (verse 5).

And those truths are only in the first five verses. There's even more. I encourage you to go read this chapter! It's one of my favorites.

Here are the statements 1 Peter 2 gives regarding those who believe in Jesus Christ as their Savior.

1. We are chosen (verse 9).
2. We are a royal priesthood (verse 9).
3. We are a holy nation (verse 9).
4. We are God's possession (verse 9).
5. We are called out of darkness into His marvelous light (verse 9).
6. We are God's people (verse 10).
7. We have received mercy (verse 10).

If I ever start to doubt my worth and find my joy disappearing, I remind myself of these eighteen statements. I encourage you to study them in depth so you can discover what they mean and how they apply to you!

Attack!

It's time to attack! Well, not really. But we can go on the offensive (or play offense) by following Paul's advice in Romans 12:9-21. He describes how to live as a new creation in Christ, as a living sacrifice to God. These guidelines have become an emergency toolkit for days when my joy is threatened. When I am tempted to hand over my joy, I hand these over instead.

Love (verse 10)

Paul says to "love one another with brotherly affection." So, when someone I know is unkind to me, I aim to be kind and say hello to them. I may even write a note or get them their favorite treat. Showing love in ways personal to them is best. If they like gifts, give a little something. If they like encouragement, send them a note.

When my husband has done something that hurts me, my stubborn sin-driven will wants to hurt him back. But I've found that one of the quickest ways to mend my frustration and my hurt is to serve him, to show him love. So, since I know that he loves to come home to a clean house I spend some time cleaning even though I really want to make it a mess instead.

Our natural response to those trying to hurt us or steal our joy will be revenge. Our joy-filled response instead motivates us to do the opposite. The options of how you love one another are vast. Get creative with it.

Honor (verse 10)

I love this verse for saying, "Outdo one another in showing honor." You know those people who always try to one-up you? Well, now you get to play that role. Go above and beyond what would normally be expected.

What does it look like to honor someone? You speak highly of them. You put that person and their concerns before your own. You respect and esteem them. I know this is asking a lot. It is hard to respect someone who is unkind. But think of an elder, like a grandmother or grandfather. There is a certain respect and honor you show them, even if you disagree with them. That's what we need to do here.

Hospitality (verse 13)

It's easy to "show hospitality" to our friends, inviting them over for dinner or out to lunch. But our enemy? Forget it. But one of the best ways to love someone and honor a person is to be hospitable.

Showing hospitality is saying, "You're important and valuable." Each one of us was created by God in His image. Being hospitable means showing you recognize this truth. So, invite them to lunch. Take care of their needs. Bring them their favorite drink. Offer them a ride if they need it. Show them their worth in Christ, even if they don't know it themselves.

Empathy (verse 15)

We are all going through difficult times. Not one of us is immune to hardships. Paul says in this verse we are to "rejoice with those who rejoice [and] weep with those who weep." Listen to their stories. If they just had a baby or grandbaby, celebrate with them. If someone in their life just experienced a heart attack, weep with them. Pray for them.

I'm not a fan of the "fake it till you make it" slogan. But I also know it's hard to care about someone who doesn't care about you at all. This is a great time for an honest conversation with God, admitting you are powerless to love others in this way. Ask Him to supply empathy and compassion so you don't have to fake it. Then you may step out in faith, not your feelings, to act according to what you know is true. He can supply you with love, empathy, and compassion for others as you see them from His perspective.

Truce (verse 18-19)

This one can be tricky. Seek peace, not revenge. This is challenging, especially if they've been mean and callous. "If possible, so far as it depends on you, live peaceably with all," means there will be times when the other person will not let you resolve a tension. You are not responsible for the outcome. You are only responsible for your contribution to the end goal of peace.

This may include offering a truce, even if it is a quiet treaty within the mind. Remind yourself of the bigger picture and the bigger objective. I walk into a situation saying to myself, "No matter what they say, no matter what they do, I'm not going to fight back. I'm going to do whatever is necessary for peace to be present."

You don't need to compromise your beliefs or your values. But you might have to mix some of their ideas in with yours. I can be stubborn and insistent when I think I have the best idea. Even though my idea might be good, other's ideas are pretty good too. And their solution will work well, just look a little different. So, going with their idea, rather than insisting on mine or offering a mix of the two ideas allows for peace rather than tension.

You need to decide what this looks like in your situation. It will most likely look different for everyone, but if your big picture is present and you're seeking peace rather than their demise, then you're on the right track.

I have only touched on five of the behaviors Paul lays out to coach us as believers. Start with these five, then add even more as you progress. There are so many ways we can apply Scripture to our lives in a practical way. This is one of them. Read Romans 12 and find your inspiration. Before you know it, your toolkit will overflow, and people will no longer stand as a threat to your joy.

People Can Bring Us Joy

I never used to do any of the above. When confronted by someone who was attempting to steal my joy, I would simply avoid them. It was the easiest solution. But easiest wasn't the best in this situation because the easiest option didn't add joy to my life. It drained it even faster. So, I don't avoid people anymore. When I come into the conversation or the situation with the right mindset, a mindset of love and honor, I'm good. In fact, I'm more than good. Because the truth is people are also a great source of joy!

Paul says repeatedly in his letters that people are his source of joy. 2 Timothy 1:4 says, "I long to see you, that I may be filled with joy." And in 1 Thessalonians 2:20, he says, "For you are our glory and joy." In Philippians 1, he says his prayers are filled with joy because he's praying for the believers in Philippi. And in the second chapter he says his joy would be complete if they would be of the same mind as one another.

Over and over again Paul mentions how his joy is made more abundant because of the people in his life and their love for God.

My Joy Is Not for Sale

One of the moms I worked with at the kids' school was very condescending and rude. She always dismissed my ideas and interrupted any time I tried to speak. One day it really affected me, and my daughter found me crying in my room. She was concerned and asked why I was crying. I told her that someone had said some mean things and I was a little hurt. She replied, "Mommy, remember Punchinello? The stickers only stick if you let them." She was referring to one of the stories I read to them often, *You Are Special* by Max Lucado.[20]

It's the story of Punchinello, Lucia, and the Wemmicks (wooden people). It has such a great message about perspective and the importance of spending time with God. If you haven't read it, please do. It's something special.

Punchinello was a little guy who was covered in gray dot stickers placed there by others because they did not think Punchinello was a good Wemmick. He learns he has control over whether the hurt and pain inflicted by others will stick to him or not. The stickers only stuck to him because he valued the opinion of the person placing the sticker.

My daughter reminded me that joy has a similar truth. We have control over whether our cup has holes and whether we'll allow people to affect our joy. The joy only leaks from your cup if you allow it. No person or circumstance can take it. You are the only one who can give up your joy. It's only theirs if you hand it over.

So, take a stance today. Look at whatever is puncturing your cup, whether it's a person, a circumstance, or a health issue, and say forcibly, "My joy. Is not. For sale."

CHAPTER EIGHT

Hidden Dangers

You can't have a soul filled with joy if your soul is filled with something else! That may seem obvious, but it wasn't always to me.

"Pride goeth before the fall." This renowned maxim paraphrases a verse in Proverbs. "Pride goes before destruction, and a haughty spirit before a fall" (Proverbs 16:18). This verse has served as a commentary for my life more times than I'd like to admit. Pride has gotten me in trouble so many times. It's something I've been working on. It's not my desire to be prideful. Yet it sneaks up on me, and before I realize it, I've done or said something that came from a position of pride rather than humility. Am I the only one who has thought they knew best?

One summer I dropped my kids off at summer camp. I took my daughter and the other girls from our church to the swimming pool for the swim test. The lifeguard asked them to swim from one side to the other using front crawl without touching the bottom.

My daughter was concerned because front crawl is not her preferred way of swimming. She prefers to be a mermaid. But I assured her that she would be okay. "You'll be fine. Just do your best."

She got in the pool and swam. She did a decent job. She's not going to win any Olympic medals, but she swam across the pool without touching the bottom as requested. She got out, and the lifeguard gave her a shallow band, meaning she didn't pass the test. This mama was not happy.

Here's a little backstory. I grew up at this same camp and fell in love with everything water-related during a waterfront class in junior high. I became a lifeguard and swim instructor for this camp, and I also guarded and taught at a local community college. I loved it so much I taught private swim lessons for over fifteen years. I know my daughter is a safe swimmer, and I trust her in the pool.

Now, back to camp. When the lifeguard failed my daughter, I asked if she could try again. The lifeguard ignored me at first. I asked what my daughter should have done differently to pass, and the lifeguard said, "I told her to swim across the pool using front crawl without touching the bottom."

My daughter looked at me and said in a shaky voice, "I didn't touch the bottom, Mom."

So, I asked again, "Can she try again? What does she need to do differently?"

The lifeguard responded forcefully. "In my opinion she is not strong enough. But we can work with her throughout the week to get her stronger."

Now this was a very professional, well-said answer. The lifeguard handled herself very well. I think back to the times I had a parent question my judgment, and I know I wasn't as polished with my answer.

But my pride didn't accept this answer. My pride heard that this lifeguard's opinion was different than mine, so it must be wrong. This lifeguard didn't know any of my background. She didn't know I had conducted these same exact swim tests hundreds of times before she was even born. She didn't know my credentials, and I'm glad I had enough forethought to keep them to myself.

Paul the apostle has a moment in his letter to the church of Philippi (Philippians 3) where he talks about his credentials. He says that when it comes to credentials, he has them. He was circumcised, a member of the tribe of Benjamin, a Pharisee, a Hebrew of Hebrews, blameless under the law. He says in verse 7, "But whatever gain I had, I counted as loss for the sake of Christ." He didn't go around boasting in himself. Everything he did was to point people to Jesus. He counted his credentials as loss for the sake of Christ.

He continues in verse 8. "Indeed, I count everything as loss because of the surpassing worth of knowing Christ Jesus my Lord. For his sake I have suffered the loss of all things and count them as rubbish, in order that I may gain Christ."

In that moment I was filled with pride and wanted to say to this lifeguard, "Do you know who I am? Do you know my credentials? I know my daughter can swim." But my mind should have been more concerned with proclaiming the name of Jesus in a gracious and humble response. I allowed my pride to alter my thoughts and my actions. As I got into the car to drive away, I knew I hadn't glorified Jesus. I didn't proclaim the humility of Christ. I showed pride of spirit instead. I didn't like how I acted.

Pride

Pride can get us into all sorts of trouble. Pride is the seed of arrogance, judgment, and jealousy. Remember when Saul became jealous of David when the women sang his praises after the battles? "Saul has struck down his thousands and David his ten thousands" (1 Samuel 18:7). Jealousy completely corrupted him, and it does the same to us.

Why do we get upset or jealous when someone else is successful? It's like we're saying that both of us can't be successful at the same time. Why can't we both live out our dream? When did it become okay to teach the lesson that if they succeed, I won't or can't?

Why can't we all succeed? Why does it have to be them or us? Why can't I be excited and happy for my friends' successes? Am I afraid my own God-given gifts will be rendered worthless if others use their gifts to their full potential? When I put it that way, it sounds kind of silly. But that is exactly what we're doing when we are filled with pride: thinking of ourselves rather than others. Joy doesn't have room for jealousy and pride.

I watched a beautiful display of compassion on *The Today Show* once. Dylan Dreyer, meteorologist and host, shared with the viewers that she recently had a miscarriage. Moments later her coworker and fellow host, Jenna Bush Hager, announced her pregnancy. Jenna felt bad announcing such great news on the same day Dylan had such sad news. Dylan replied, "My sadness does not take away from your joy."[21] This was the perfect response. There was no jealousy, no competition, and no pride. She was genuinely excited for her coworker.

She could have easily become bitter or jealous or mean. But she chose compassion instead. Jealousy ceases when we rejoice with others. Pride ends when we really see others and consider them first.

As we drove away from camp that day after my daughter's swim test, I turned to God's Word for correction and encouragement. I looked up different verses about pride. As I read each one, my heart knew the truth. My pride had done some damage.

Proverbs 29:23 says, "One's pride will bring him low, but he who is lowly in spirit will obtain honor." I was brought low, and my actions did not bring myself, my family, my church, or my God any honor. I wasn't horrible by the world's standards. I didn't lash out or even say anything mean. But I wasn't gracious and understanding. I made it known I disagreed with her decision. I made sure she knew my daughter was upset because of it.

My disagreement and my daughter's emotions didn't matter in that moment, though. I should have respected her authority and accepted the decision with grace rather than protest, at least in that moment. Maybe going to her later and talking about it would have been okay, but in the moment, it was not appropriate—especially because I've been there. I know what it's like to have a parent disagree with your decision. Because of my credentials I should have been more gracious and understanding, but instead I let my experience give me a haughty spirit, and I didn't shine Jesus brightly at all.

It's likely that's what Paul meant when he said he counts it all rubbish for the sake of knowing Christ. I know Christ, and it doesn't mean my credentials are worthless. It means that in the moment I should have put Christ before my qualifications and my pride. Instead, I chose pride over Christ. Knowing Christ intimately results in being like Christ, and I failed in that moment.

Guilt vs. Shame

I'm sure you've heard the phrase "I'm ashamed of myself." I know I was ashamed of how I acted with the lifeguard. I have realized that sometimes as pride begins to fall away, shame can take its place. We see our error, and we feel shame. But shame is not of God. And it's dangerous.

When I get angry and yell at my kids, knowing I could do better, shame creeps in. Lies consume my mind. *You're horrible. You're the worst. The kids are going to be scarred for life.* But those thoughts come from the evil one. These statements condemn me as a mom.

Guilt, however, doesn't condemn me. It speaks the truth. It brings the truth to light. I was wrong to yell at my kids. But I am not a horrible mom because I did it. Guilt is linked to my actions and can be forgiven. Shame is linked to my identity and is a lie.

My immediate thought after I yell is *I shouldn't have done that,* and that thought was put there by the Holy Spirit. He shows me my guilt. But guilt is different from shame.

Guilt means feeling bad about something we've done. Shame means feeling bad about who we are. Guilt says, "I did something bad." Shame says, "I am bad."

Guilt is brought on because the Holy Spirit is convicting us of our sin. We have done something against the Lord. We need to repent and turn the other way. Guilt leads to confession, which leads to freedom.

Shame, on the other hand, is not something that comes from the Holy Spirit. Shame means feeling bad about who you are. It reshapes your identity. What we've done or what's been done to us becomes a label we either see and portray to others or that others see and project onto us. We are no longer identified by our name but instead by our new label: adulterer, rape victim, the lady with the anger problem, or addict, to name a few.

I think of the woman brought before Jesus because of her sins (John 8). We don't know her name. Yet, two thousand years later we are still talking about her story (for good reason). She was the woman caught in the act of adultery. We have so many labels we give each other. Some are true, and some aren't. If I said the name Hester, you may or may not know who I'm talking about. But if I say, "The scarlet letter," you most likely know exactly what I'm referencing.

In the book *The Scarlet Letter,* Hester is the main character.[22] She was caught in adultery and forced to wear a scarlet "A" on the outside of her clothing as a reminder of her sinful act. We are probably more familiar with the scarlet letter than the name of the main character. Do you feel this way sometimes? Do you feel people look at you and see your past actions rather than the real you? Does it feel like everyone is looking at your scarlet letter rather than your face?

Maybe you are experiencing shame right now. Maybe, like me, you can't shake the feeling of deep embarrassment and shame you carry from your past. If I am describing your story or getting close to the feelings you have right now, let me say there is hope. Joy is still possible.

I remember the months following my discovery of how I had treated people with my pride-filled, bossy tone. My joy was gone. I felt like a horrible human being. I felt I didn't deserve to be in leadership. I thought people would be in better hands with someone else at the helm. Intellectually I knew I needed to keep studying God's Word and praying through it all, but my joy was long gone. I was sinking into a state of loneliness and despair.

I realized my shame was linked to who I thought I was, not who God says I am. I was allowing Satan to define my identity through my shame. I had allowed myself to believe I was a horrible person because I had treated people horribly. But I realized God had redeemed me just as He has redeemed others.

God said in Isaiah 43 that I am His. I am precious to Him, and He calls me by name, not because I'm someone special or because I'm perfect but because I am His child for whom

His Son died to take away that very shame I was feeling. I can declare I am not who my shame says I am.

I did treat people horribly, but I am not a horrible person because of that. I confessed my sin. I was forgiven. Shame anchors me in the past, but God's forgiveness leads me into the future with possibility and promise.

Pride, guilt, and shame will all hinder our joy. If you are struggling today, here are some things you can work through to mend your cup and fill it with joy.

Admit It

The first step toward joy is admitting our sin. I had to bring my pride before God. I had to truly repent of my sin. I'm guilty of thinking it is enough to acknowledge my sin. I tell myself, "I know I struggle with pride. It's a weakness of mine," and then I continue on my way, believing acknowledgement is the same as repentance. Am I the only one? I excuse the sin away or hide it. But this belief is far from truth.

Excusing sin or hiding sin isn't the way to mend our cups. The sin will puncture holes in your cup, even if you can't see it or if you convince yourself it's okay. Joy isn't possible without repentance.

Seek Forgiveness from God

"For godly grief produces a repentance that leads to salvation without regret, whereas worldly grief produces death" (2 Corinthians 7:10). Godly grief occurs when we have sorrow over our sin. When someone wants to trust Jesus as their Savior for the first time, there is an admittance of guilt. We must identify ourselves as sinners in need of a Savior. Godly grief occurs, which motivates us to ask for forgiveness and trust Jesus as our Savior. This sorrow over our sin produces true repentance, and that repentance leads to our salvation.

And although we can never do anything to lose our salvation (Romans 8:30), we must have godly grief over our daily sin. As a believer my sins grieve God, and my sins should grieve me as well because they place a barrier between God and me. Seeking forgiveness daily from God allows for unhindered communion with Him.

Seek Forgiveness from Others

Next, we must ask forgiveness from those we've sinned against. If I'm honest, I'm not a fan of this step. Matthew 5:23 talks about this in the context of anger. Before we can present our sacrifices—our worship—to God, we must make things right with the people we've wronged.

I remember attending a baby-gender-reveal party for a friend. A mutual friend was there, and I had been unkind to this mutual friend in the past. I was jealous of her and her ability to accomplish things that I had been trying to accomplish for years. My pride couldn't believe someone else could come in and do it better than me. So, I had the opportunity at this party to come face to face with her and ask for her forgiveness. I admitted I had not treated her with kindness and that my actions had all stemmed from pride and jealousy. She graciously accepted my apology and offered her forgiveness.

It was one of the hardest things I have ever done but it was also one of the most freeing moments in my life. A huge weight was lifted and the joy I had been missing gradually returned. God still had some more transforming to do in me before I could really embrace a joy-filled soul, but in that moment a few of the holes in my cup were mended.

It's important to confess our wrongs to both God and the people we've wronged—when it is possible and safe—and ask for their forgiveness. Though it is incredibly hard to do, it's necessary. True joy will not come otherwise.

Make a Change

Now it's time to make a change. This is the heart of true repentance. Ephesians 4:22-24 says "to put off your old self, which belongs to your former manner of life and is corrupt through deceitful desires, and to be renewed in the spirit of your minds, and to put on the new self, created after the likeness of God in true righteousness and holiness."

Repentance is more than confessing and clearing our conscience. Our attitude toward sin needs to change. The great news is you don't have to make the change all on your own. If it was up to me and my human will, I would fail every time. But because I have the Holy Spirit guiding me and helping me along the way, I'm able to have patience and talk with kindness and be calm with my kids. I still mess up, but I do so less and less.

Jesus said to the woman caught in adultery, "Neither do I condemn you; go, and from now on sin no more" (John 8:11). Jesus didn't condemn her. But He did ask her to make a change. He told her to turn away from her sin. Jesus doesn't condemn you either (Romans 8:1), but we must make a change as well. And with the help of the Holy Spirit and a renewal of our thoughts, it's possible.

Take Your Shame to Jesus and Accept His Forgiveness

Here's an incredible truth about the story of the woman caught in adultery. The men brought her before Jesus to bring shame to her and her family. We don't know the details of the offense. We don't know her name or the names of her accusers. We do know the men intended to shame her, but Jesus granted forgiveness instead.

Shame is something humans give to other humans (or to oneself). It does not come from God. Jesus did not shame this woman. He didn't even shame the men. He pointed out their own guilt but brought no shame.

If we don't accept God's forgiveness, we will replace our guilt with shame. We can know we have been forgiven without accepting it. When that happens, shame takes the space that guilt once held.

As women we can be very judgmental. And almost always we judge ourselves more harshly than others. James 2:13 says that "mercy triumphs over judgment." The judge in my head needs to submit to the real judge, who is on the throne—God Himself. Colossians 3:15 commands us to let the peace of Christ rule, not our feelings. God's mercy and forgiveness truly trump any judgment we can give ourselves.

There are many people out in the world who believe we feel shame because we haven't forgiven ourselves, even if we believe God has forgiven us. I disagree with this. It is not biblical. Forgiveness must come from the offended. The offender can't offer forgiveness. Forgiveness cancels a debt. If I have wronged you, I am now indebted to you. I can't cancel my own debt. It simply doesn't make sense.

What we can do, however, is accept God's forgiveness. He died on the cross for us. He offered Himself and has forgiven us (John 3:16; Ephesians 1:7; 1 John 1:9). I don't need to forgive myself; I need to accept God's forgiveness and allow it to take the place of both guilt and shame. Accept His forgiveness today, friend. Leave your guilt and shame at the cross and embrace your identity in Christ.

I know some of you reading this book have shame, not because of something you've done but because of something done to you. Maybe child abuse made you feel worthless. Perhaps rape or sexual abuse took away all your dignity. It was not your fault, yet the lies you've been listening to for so long say you did something wrong.

It's time to free yourself from that shame. The woman caught in adultery is no longer the woman caught in adultery. That's not her identity any longer. She is the woman redeemed by Christ. She is the woman rescued by Jesus. The addict is not a recovering addict but a child of God pulled out of the pit of despair. The girl sexually abused by her uncle is free from the lie that says she is damaged goods. She is now whole and perfect, set free by Jesus.

Our identity is found in Jesus, not what we've done or what's been done to us. I don't have to be known as the mean, proud lady. I am redeemed. And even if people still think that about me, my identity is not wrapped up in their opinions. I know who I am in Christ. I know I am a new creation and that Jesus's transformation in me is real, true, and constant. It doesn't matter what those people think.

Getting to that point was difficult. God used His Word and some very dear friends to affirm what I was learning in my study of Scripture. They came alongside me and listened to my feelings of shame. They held me gently as I shared the deepest parts of myself. Making myself vulnerable was scary, but it allowed me to release my shame and get a tangible hug from God. They affirmed my identity in Christ, and through their love I felt God's love.

Releasing my shame and accepting God's forgiveness and mercy mended my cup, and my soul overflowed with joy as a result!

CHAPTER NINE

Do Unto Others

I can't write a book about joy without discussing the topic of forgiving others. I believe we can never experience joy to the full extent God intended so long as there is unforgiveness in our hearts.

Up until a few years ago, I would have said forgiveness is sometimes hard but always possible. Then I ended up in a conflict with some friends, and everything I previously felt towards forgiveness got tangled up in very difficult feelings. I stood at a crossroads. Do I believe what I have always taught and know God's Word says, or do I sit in my unforgiveness because forgiveness seems impossible?

I was angry—really angry. And that anger kept me from doing what I could to reach out to these friends. But I couldn't in that moment. I was paralyzed in my anger and confusion. And in that paralysis I lost all my joy, which in turn made the anger worse. It felt like they were the enemy, stealing everything from me. Friendships. Truth. Joy.

About two months later it was time for a new Bible study to start at my church. To be honest, I didn't really want to do it. But my personal time with the Lord was starting to struggle, and I needed the accountability. I didn't know what the study was, and I didn't really care. I only knew that I needed to maintain good grounding, so I signed up for the study.

On the first night they passed out the books. I looked down and it read, "Joseph: The Journey to Forgiveness."[23] I wanted to jump out of my seat right there and run. I thought, *Absolutely no. Not going to happen.* I knew forgiveness was what the Lord wanted from me, but I was not ready. And honestly, I didn't know if I'd ever be ready to forgive.

Have you ever been in a situation like this? I think of stories I've read about where the parents of a child who has been killed speak with the murderer and forgive him or her. I'd like to say I would be able to do the same thing, but I'm not so sure. Forgive the person who took my baby's life?

I know each of you reading this have had circumstances that brought you to a crossroads of forgiveness. Maybe you're like me, and it's a crossroads forced upon you by betrayal. Or maybe you're the parent I just spoke of that has lost a child at the hands of someone or something else, and the choice to forgive is unfathomable. Or maybe you're facing a different circumstance where you have been hurt deeply by someone, and you simply can't forgive them. You think, "They don't deserve my forgiveness."

I've been there. I didn't realize it until I worked through this Bible study, but I operated on the underlying belief that if I forgive someone for something, I am condoning what they did, saying it was okay. I subconsciously was saying "no" to forgiveness because I didn't want to excuse their action. I was still grieving the loss of a friendship. I was still grieving the hurtful words that had been said.

What began the transformation in me was a little parable Jesus shared with His disciples. It's found in Matthew 18. I encourage you to read it for yourself, but here's the story with a modern twist.

There are three women. One woman, we'll call her Shelly, owes money to another woman. We'll call her Danielle. The time is up for Shelly to repay the loan to Danielle. She owes over one million dollars. Danielle has every right to throw Shelly in prison or even have her killed because of her inability to pay the debt. Instead, Danielle cancels the debt. Shelly is completely forgiven and does not have to pay one more penny of the million owed. Shelly leaves the meeting stunned but relieved. On her way home Shelly runs into her neighbor. We'll call her Margaret. Margaret owes Shelly ten dollars she borrowed a few weeks back. Shelly calls the cops and has Margaret arrested because she's unable to pay back the money owed.

One woman owed a million dollars, and the other only owed ten. The one who was forgiven turned around and denied forgiveness to the another.

As I read through this story, my eyes filled with tears, and I was overcome with grief. I had heard and read this parable before, but that night as I read through this story during my Bible study homework, the Holy Spirit convicted my heart, and the story became so real to me. How could I hold a grudge against someone when Jesus has forgiven all my debt a million times over? Jesus has forgiven every single one of my sins.

Forgiveness was the only possible response. I wasn't admitting the wrongs done to me didn't matter or didn't hurt. I was declaring that Jesus's sacrifice on the cross for both of us mattered more. I was forgiven on that cross, and so were those who hurt me. Second Corinthians 5:21 says, "For our sake he made him to be sin who knew no sin, so that in him we might become the righteousness of God." We are declared righteous and forgiven because Jesus took our place.

In order to forgive others, we need to receive His complete forgiveness. If He gave us complete forgiveness, who are we to deny forgiveness to someone else?

Forgiveness is not saying what they did is okay, nor is it condoning the wrong. Forgiveness is not saying the hurt is healed.

Forgiveness is saying, "You don't owe me anymore." Forgiveness is releasing anger or resentment held against someone. It's not being best friends with a person. That's reconciliation. Forgiveness is recognizing our own sin that has been washed in the blood of Jesus Christ. We don't deserve the forgiveness that came on the cross. Yet, He gave it. The people that have hurt me and the people that have hurt you may not deserve our forgiveness. Yet, if we believe in Jesus, we must give it.

We don't know how quickly Joseph forgave his brothers after they sold him into slavery (Genesis 37). Maybe it happened right away, or maybe it was more of a journey, a journey that took him through some experiences. God used those experiences to heal him and shape him into the man who saved Egypt and forgave the brothers who betrayed him.

Forgiveness has been a journey for me as well. It didn't happen overnight. There are still days when it hurts. There are still days when I feel those negative emotions attempt a comeback. There are days when my heart still hurts. I wonder how my friends can still be friends with those who were so mean and cut such deep wounds. It's a process. It's a daily surrendering of my will to Jesus. My will says it's not fair. My heart wants to cut everyone out because it hurts too much.

But Jesus has asked me to forgive. Jesus has asked me to love anyway. Jesus has asked me to reconcile. And so, I've spent hours praying for my heart and for those who hurt my heart. Little by little Jesus has softened me. I'll admit I'm not completely there. I used to feel a stab in the heart every time their name was mentioned, and my lungs forgot how to breathe. But now it's only a twinge.

My prayer is that someday there won't be any hurt left at all. Of course, I wanted to have it happen right away. I wanted to be a "perfect" example of Christ and forgive and reconcile immediately, having only love for them from day one. But it didn't happen. I wrestled with God through it. Through tears I begged Him to take away the hurt and the anger. Through tears I begged Him to reverse the clock and tell me how to change everything and salvage everything. Through tears I begged Him to give me a heart of gold that would allow me to love despite everything. I wanted instant results.

I've learned transformation is a process. If it would have happened all in one night, then the lessons I've learned in the waiting and praying wouldn't have happened. The dependence on my Lord for His outpouring of the fruit of His Spirit would have never occurred.

I realized my friends aren't the enemy. Ephesians 6:12 says, "For we do not wrestle against flesh and blood, but against the rulers, against the authorities, against the cosmic powers over this present darkness, against the spiritual forces of evil in the heavenly places."

I can now look back and see why they did what they did. I don't agree with what they did, and I probably never will. But I can see where they were coming from, and I can empathize with their response. And what's more, I can honestly say I love them. Not because of what they did or what I've done. It's because Jesus loves them. It's because Jesus forgave me, and He's forgiven them too!

Misplacing Blame

Sometimes hurt comes because of a person, and we place our anger towards them. And sometimes we direct it toward

God. It's easy to blame God because we expect everything to be perfect through Him. He is good. He is love. So, when things happen in our lives that aren't loving or good, we blame God for it. Why wasn't He there to protect me? Why did He let them die? Where was God when...?

There's an episode of *Little House on the Prairie* when Mr. Edwards has given up on believing in God because He blames God for not healing his wife and daughter. Mrs. Ingalls says, "You're blaming God, and until you stop blaming Him, you continue to live in the past and have no future."[24] It's true. God didn't cause things to happen to us. He didn't stop them, but it's not His job to stop them. And as long as we place blame on God (or others), we can not move forward.

Naomi blamed God for her troubles (Ruth 1). Many theologians have varying views on the hardships Naomi faced. Some say she and her husband brought it upon themselves because they left their land and went to a land whose people worshipped foreign gods. Some say they had no choice because of the famine, and God led them to Moab. Whatever camp you fall into, Naomi allowed her situation to build up bitterness in her soul to the point she changed her name to Mara (meaning bitter) to reflect her new disposition (Ruth 1:20).

Has bitterness worked its way so deep into your heart that your name has changed? Is your public persona different from the real you? Do you blame God for what has happened to you?

God will allow things to happen to help us see our need for Him. But "we know that for those who love God all things work together for good, for those who are called according to his purpose" (Romans 8:28). Amid Naomi's sorrow over her sons and husband, God provided for her by bringing Ruth into her life. He also set the stage for provision down the road by lining up Boaz to care for them both.

Naomi blinded herself to these blessings. She was set on living in bitterness rather than having joy in her relationship with Ruth or being thankful for the things and people she did have. I don't presume to think I would have acted any differently than Naomi did, but the truth remains. I wonder what Naomi's level of joy would have been if she had a grateful attitude rather than a bitter one.

Have you been hurt? Are you struggling to forgive someone? Have you allowed bitterness to take root? Our feelings can go so deep into our soul that they are hard to face and harder to release. But if we allow anger and unforgiveness to fester and bitterness to take root, our cups will shatter, and there won't be anything to fill with joy! Are you on a journey to forgiveness but don't know how to get there? Here are a few things you can do right now that might help.

Recognize God's Presence

God walked in the garden with Adam and Eve. After sin entered the picture, He could no longer walk with them, though He longed to do so. He devised another way. The Ark of the Covenant allowed God to dwell with His children once again. Then Jesus came and walked among us. And now, the Holy Spirit is with us everywhere we go.

You may not feel that God is near, but He is. He may not be showing up as a pillar of fire as He did for the Israelites, but He is with us. He uses people in our lives to care for us.

A friend of mine left her house as soon as she turned eighteen because of the abuse occurring there. She wasn't safe, and she knew she had to leave. But she didn't have much money. Her part-time, minimum-wage job rarely provided enough for food after the rent was paid. Her neighbor, who was a young girl herself, came over a couple times a month with a bag full of food that she took from her pantry at home.

The crazy thing is my friend never once said she was hungry or didn't have any food. The neighbor didn't know her situation. She just wanted to give my friend some food.

Looking back, my friend knows without a doubt that God provided for her through this little girl. God was present even though she didn't recognize it at the time. He hadn't forgotten about her or her situation. He was with her through it all just as He was with Naomi, and He is with you too.

Realize You Have Been Forgiven Much

> He has delivered us from the domain of darkness and transferred us to the kingdom of his beloved Son, in whom we have redemption, the forgiveness of sins.
>
> —Colossians 1:13-14

Jesus has forgiven us—for everything! We can have redemption because of His death. He didn't die only to cover your little white lies. Though those are included, He died to forgive you for everything you think, say, or do that keeps you from a holy God. We are no longer in darkness; we are in His kingdom.

The law shows us we will never measure up. Jesus shows us we don't have to. We don't have to be perfect. We don't have to make the right decisions all the time to be accepted. That's what grace is all about. As Jesus hung on the cross in our place, He made it so we can come directly to God and have fellowship with Him. We are forgiven!

One thing that can help you visualize how much you are forgiven is a "debt list." Write down everything you can think of for which you've been forgiven by God. If you're honest and specific, this could be a very long list. Mine was! Once you've done it, take a good, long look at the list. God has cancelled every single one of those debts.

Respond to That Forgiveness by Forgiving Others

In order to forgive others, I had to see the people who hurt me the same way Jesus saw me as He hung on the cross. They are His children just as I am. He loves them as much as He loves me. He has forgiven them as He has forgiven me.

Take the debt list you made and write in another column all the things done by the person who hurt you. These are the debts they have against you. Once you're done, look at the list. Do you notice the difference? Odds are the length of your debts is greater than the list of debts waiting to be forgiven by you.

We don't have to forgive others for God to forgive us. But if we choose not to forgive someone, it might be we truly don't understand the depths we were forgiven.

Put on then, as God's chosen ones, holy and beloved, compassionate hearts, kindness, humility, meekness, and patience, bearing with one another and, if one has a complaint against another, forgiving each other; as the Lord has forgiven you, so you also must forgive. And above all these put on love, which binds everything together in perfect harmony. And let the peace of Christ rule in your hearts, to which indeed you were called in one body. And be thankful.

—Colossians 3:12-15

If we are adding all these things to our lives, they will choke out bitterness and unforgiveness. When I have a compassionate heart, act with kindness, think of others before myself, and show them patience, then forgiveness will naturally follow.

Remember to Pray

Cover the situation in prayer from all sides. Ask God to search your own heart to see if there is any part you have to play. Ask God to give you discernment and wisdom but be careful to resist asking God to show the other person where they were wrong. It's tempting to ask God to show them the error of their ways. Instead, ask God to help you develop a love for the other person. It may take time for love to develop, but God will answer your prayer.

Also, pray for the friend or pastor guiding you through this that they will have discernment and wisdom as they counsel you. Ask God also that He will reveal His truth to you as you study His Word.

I know from experience that if you are seeking God, sincerely asking for His help to forgive, He will show up and blow you away. I never thought I could love the ones who hurt me. The knife of betrayal and hurtful words cut so deeply I didn't think love would ever be possible again. But the more I prayed over the situation and prayed for the ones who hurt me, the more love began to break through.

It's possible, friend. Continue to pursue God, and He will show you the way.

If you are still struggling with forgiveness, dig deeper into God's Word for truth and discernment. Start with Matthew 18. Read it. Study it. Join a Bible study group or invite others to go through a study with you.

Next, study the life of Joseph in Genesis 37-50. These chapters lead you through his life and the many people who wronged him, showing Joseph's path to forgiveness. Colossians chapters 2 and 3 are also rich in truths about forgiveness. As you study, reach out to your pastor or a trusted friend who knows God's Word and ask for guidance. Forgiveness is one of the most difficult things we must do, but it is also one of the most liberating!

One Last Thing About Forgiveness

That night as I read through the parable Jesus taught about forgiveness, I repented of my unforgiveness and anger. And then I forgave those who hurt me. I cried and prayed and laid everything before Jesus. I felt love for the first time in a long time, and the weight of unforgiveness lifted from me. I could breathe deeper.

However, the hurt I felt did not disappear. It's been a while now, and I still have some hurt feelings that rise in my soul when I think of the people involved.

I battled with this for a while. Did the hurt mean my forgiveness wasn't genuine? Did it mean I needed to forgive again? I wrestled with this for a long time and realized something. Wounds take time to heal.

Trauma, like suffered in a car accident, can cause your physical heart to be wounded, requiring surgery. The doctors go in and repair the damage. After surgery the doctor says you need to take it easy because your body is still healing from the trauma.

God performed surgery on my heart when He led me to forgiveness. I couldn't do it on my own. God corrected my heart. He made it new again. But I still had to recover from the trauma and the surgery. My body took time to heal, and I still have a scar.

So, what happens when feelings of anger rise when I hear their name? It caught me off guard the first couple times. Wasn't my anger supposed to be gone now that I forgave them? I knew my forgiveness was real, so why was I struggling?

I don't know about you, but I am exceptionally good at letting things fester. I turn things over and over in my mind until they are five times bigger and meaner. I dwell on issues. They captivate my mind, and I think of nothing else. That's why taking every thought captive according to the Word of God (2 Corinthians 10:5) is so important.

I know the truth in His Word because I've studied it. I know what anger will do to my joy. I know what God has done for me and for them. I know the truth, so I must make sure I'm thinking about those truths rather than the lies the devil would like me to believe (which is causing the anger).

> Finally, brothers, whatever is true, whatever is honorable, whatever is just, whatever is pure, whatever is lovely, whatever is commendable, if there is any excellence, if there is anything worthy of praise, think about these things.
>
> —Philippians 4:8

And when I struggle to think of these things because my feelings take over, I ask the Lord for help. We can see these lingering feelings as prompts to continue to take it to the Lord in prayer. "Lord, You tell me to pray for my enemies and love those who have hurt me. Lord, I want nothing more than to love those whom You love and see them the way You see them. Guide me today, Lord. Give me Your perspective about the situation and the people. Help me to continue taking my thoughts captive, to dwell in Your truths, and to rest in Your love. Amen."

It may take time to move on from the situation. Don't lose heart. Don't give up. Don't grow weary. The overflowing joy that comes from the journey through forgiveness is worth it.

CHAPTER TEN

Cinderella

Did you dream of being a princess when you were little? I sure did. My elementary years were flooded with new Disney princesses. It wasn't only Cinderella and Snow White anymore. We were introduced to Ariel and Jasmine and Belle. My friend and I used to pretend to be mermaids in her grandma's pool every summer. And I longed to visit a library where I could climb a ladder and ride it around the room. I knew every word to every song those princesses sang. I still do.

So, when Disney began remaking all my childhood favorites in live action, I knew I would have to see each one. *Cinderella* was up first (2015).[25] It was incredible. I love the backstories they added for the characters. We begin to learn about their "why."

Perhaps my favorite scene was the conversation between Ella as a young girl and her mother. Ella's name had not yet changed to Cinderella. Her mom is dying and asks to speak with Ella. I hate that this is my favorite scene because it's one of the saddest in the movie, but Ella's mom gives her daughter the best advice. She says, "Have courage and be kind." She tells Ella her kindness has power and magic. Ella grows up to be one of the kindest people in the kingdom even though she is treated so miserably by her stepmother and stepsisters. She follows her mother's advice and chooses to be courageous and kind in every moment.

That movie made me want to be a princess all over again. The poise, grace, and kindness she showed to everyone was so beautiful. There are so many times I look back at a situation and think to myself, *I should have been more like Cinderella in that moment.* I had the chance to have courage and be kind, and I failed miserably.

I used to look at kindness as optional. It was something I could add to my day if I wanted to, much like you add fries to your fast food order. But I learned if I want lasting joy, kindness can't be an add-on. It's more like a mantra or an attitude, a pair of glasses through which we view the world.

Last summer I was in a Chick-fil-A bathroom in Indiana, and there was a sign setting on a shelf. It read, "Go the extra mile. It's never crowded." I loved it so much I took a picture of it and posted it as an encouragement to my friends. It made me think. What does it mean to go the extra mile? All that came to mind was kindness. So many times, we are kind to those who are kind to us, and we stop there. But we're asked to go the extra mile.

Jesus asked us to be kind to those who are unkind to us. At the time Jesus said these words, Roman soldiers could ask anyone at any time to carry their burden for a mile (or more). We see this happen with Simon and the cross of Jesus. The soldiers were not kind in their orders and rarely thanked a Jew for helping.

So, when Jesus said, "And if anyone forces you to go one mile, go with him two miles" (Matthew 5:41), it was not an easy thing to do. No one likes to be forced to do anything, much less go above and beyond what is demanded.

I suppose that's why kindness isn't always easy. It goes against our natural desires. Yet, we are commanded repeatedly in God's Word to be kind.

The Bible is full of wisdom and guidance on how to show kindness. We talked in earlier chapters about outdoing one another with honor and loving our neighbor. These are all ways to show kindness. In addition to helping mend the holes that allow our cups to leak, being kind will also add joy.

How do we show kindness? What is kindness? Is it merely opening the door for someone or smiling and saying "hi?" It can be those things, but true kindness like Jesus talks about is more than nice gestures. Here are four facets to kindness that will give us a bigger picture, multiply our joy, and help us go the extra mile. (And yes, it spells MILE for those who like that kind of thing.)

(show) Mercy

Mercy is kindness on steroids. It's like a 3D version. It's more than mere kindness. I can open the door for someone. That's kindness. And that's a great first step. But opening the door for the lady who always talks trash about me and is rude to me, that's mercy because in the world's mind she doesn't deserve my kindness. Mercy is all about turning our backs on revenge, rejecting what we think a person deserves, and choosing to be kind anyway.

He has told you, O man, what is good; and what does the LORD require of you but to do justice, and to love kindness, and to walk humbly with your God?

Micah 6:8

Do justice and love kindness. In other words, treat people fairly and honestly and love to show mercy. Mercy and justice are always desired but not always given. We want mercy. We want a second chance. We want justice. We want to be treated fairly. Yet, I have found at least for me that giving someone a second chance can be difficult. Treating others fairly often means putting myself second and prioritizing the other person and their situation over mine.

I used to think *do* justice meant *give* justice. I love order. I love rules. I love knowing what is expected of myself and others. And when others aren't following the rules, I am usually the first to point it out. I love fighting for social justice too. That's probably why I became a social worker. I believe the Bible when it says we were all created equal and are all created in God's image. When someone is wronged, the offense must be rectified. When someone is treated unfairly, the wrong must be corrected.

I learned that *give* justice and *do* justice, though they share similarities, are different actions. To *give* justice means I am responsible for keeping things in order and making sure everyone is treated equitably. But to *do* justice means I am responsible for only myself. I am responsible for treating others equitably, but God is the one who delivers the justice when others don't do justice. I am responsible for myself, and I need to make sure I'm treating others fairly.

In thinking I was the one supposed to ensure justice, I never gave mercy much thought. Then I found myself in a position where I desired mercy to be shown to me. I had acted harshly in a few situations. After being shown the error of my ways, I made huge efforts to change. I apologized and started to focus my energy on improving my interactions with others. I was doing well, but a couple people continued to throw the incident back in my face. They wouldn't accept my apology or allow me to move on. They certainly weren't showing me any mercy. They were not willing to offer any second chances. As I sat in my room, crying and feeling sorry for myself, I realized I was longing for mercy, yet I was unwilling to give mercy. God showed me that what I so desperately desired was something I struggled so badly to give. I realized if I'm truly following God, then I must love mercy.

Releasing the situation and putting it in God's hands allows joy to fill your soul. Sometimes I want the person to get what they deserve. Sometimes I want revenge. I struggle to follow David's example in 1 Samuel 24:11-13. When David was chased by Saul, who sought to kill him, he had an opportunity to kill Saul instead. Saul was relieving himself in a cave, and David could have easily taken his life. But he knew it was God's job to bring judgment upon Saul. Saul was still his king and the authority to be respected. So, David showed mercy instead of revenge. This took courage and a complete faith in God.

Many times, instead of mercy, we respond to offenses with revenge. Someone cuts us off on the road, so we cut them off. Someone steals our parking spot and we yell at them. Someone eats your lunch out of the company refrigerator, so you dump the trash can on their desk. (This actually happened to one of my coworkers.) These acts aren't criminal. They're just mean. Showing mercy is letting it go and not seeking revenge. When we leave the justice to God in these moments, joy replaces the desire for revenge.

I'll admit sometimes I don't want to give it to God because I believe that my definition of justice is better than His. Although God is a just God, He's also a merciful God. Selfishly, I don't always want the person to receive mercy. Yet, our God loves mercy. He sent His Son to die in our place, knowing we are not worthy of His sacrifice. That is the ultimate example.

Some people might say we only need to show mercy after someone has apologized. But Romans 5:8 says Jesus died in our place while we were still sinners. So, if God showed us mercy while we were still sinners, then we should show others mercy without needing an apology first.

Mercy is something I am incredibly grateful for. I think of how many times I have been shown mercy, and I realize keeping it from someone else is unkind. Kindness and love are better than revenge. Seeing someone else live because of God's mercy is way better than watching someone live their life filled with sorrow and pain because they got what they deserved. Joy is the result of the former. Pride and misery are the result of the latter.

(be) Intentional

Going the extra mile means purposefully being kind. When we are intentional with our kindness, we go out of our way for another. It's more than merely opening the door for someone. It's thinking about the person who has been mean and cruel and figuring out how you can be kind in return.

I'll admit this is hard but so worth it. Your acts of kindness can start small. You don't have to buy gifts or perform any grand gestures. It may be as simple as smiling and saying "hi" to the hurtful person you've been ignoring. It might mean offering to help said person with a task. Or it may mean something more substantial. Only you can figure that out. But pray about being intentional with your kindness.

I started to think through ideas of how I could be intentional with my kindness to the rude, condescending parent I worked with at my kids' school. Instead of avoiding her, I started greeting her and asking her about her day. It may sound simple, but I went from intentionally avoiding her to intentionally speaking with her. That was a huge deal for me. I also began to pray with purpose for her. I made sure she was on my prayer list every day. I prayed for her relationship with Jesus, but I also prayed for my attitude, perspective, and motivations regarding her. These two actions changed my heart and our relationship. By the middle of the school year, I actually enjoyed our conversations. I learned more about her and her situation. I was reminded once again that everyone has a hard life; everyone has a story. These conversations gave me more to pray about, and I found my prayers for her changing. At the beginning my prayers were short and basic. Now, they are filled with love and compassion.

Being intentional with our kindness can cause our cup to overflow with joy and may even help us develop a reserve. So, I encourage you today to think of the person that often pierces your cup and drains your joy. Then think of three ways you can be intentional with your kindness toward them. Of course, it's not enough to think about being kind; we must put it into action. So, do one of those acts of kindness this week. Don't delay. The more you put it off, the less likely you'll actually do it. Being intentional is about doing.

Love One Another

Love is patient and kind; love does not envy or boast; it is not arrogant or rude. It does not insist on its own way; it is not irritable or resentful; it does not rejoice at wrongdoing, but rejoices with the truth. Love bears all things, believes all things, hopes all things, endures all things.

—1 Corinthians 13:4-7

These are famous verses about love from the Bible. Though many people apply this to a marriage relationship, it's not only about marriage. It applies to any relationship. Love is patient. That means if I want to show love, I must be patient with the lady in front of me at the grocery store. Love does not boast. That means I'm not rubbing my victory in my enemy's face even though it's tempting. There is no "I told you so" moment here.

Jesus commanded us to "love one another" (John 15:12). And if we obey His commands, our "joy [will] be full" (John 15:11). So, if we want our joy to be full and complete, we must be patient, kind, humble, and grateful.

If we expect to have joy and wonder why joy is missing from our lives, we must look at how we love people. Loving our enemies is hard. Sometimes even loving our loved ones is hard. But it's possible because God *is* love. We love because He first loved us. If we don't love others, then we don't know God (1 John 4:8,19). Love is hard, but I promise it's worth the effort. And if we don't love, our cups will remain empty. Joy will elude us.

(be an) Encourager

The best way to show kindness is to encourage someone else. Be their cheerleader. Help them succeed.

Have you watched *The Lord of the Rings Trilogy*? I love the spiritual lessons held in these movies. Sam is my favorite character. He was always there for Frodo even when Frodo told him not to come. Frodo said, "I'm going to Mordor alone!" And Sam replied, "Of course you are! And I'm going with you."[26] I love how he supports his friend no matter what but ensures his friend stays in the spotlight. When the ring started affecting Frodo's mind and will, Sam knew how to keep Frodo on the right path. He persuaded him, he carried him, and he knew what to do to help Frodo out of trouble. Sam made sure Frodo got to his destination whatever the cost. He is the ultimate encourager.

The awesome thing about kindness is that while we are kind to others by encouraging them, we are filled with joy. That joy encourages us in return and it also builds courage in others.

I was in a scholarship competition for which I had to sing a solo. Family was not allowed in the room; my audience comprised of the judges and other competitors. I was so scared. About fifteen other girls were there, and all I heard in the room was criticism and rude comments. If someone sang well, they snickered and commented on her appearance. If someone sang off key, the other girls laughed. All the girls did this except one. She was kind. She sat next to me and eased my fears. She encouraged me to give it my best, and when I finished, she cheered the loudest. Her encouragement showed her kind heart. And it gave me courage to sing my best regardless of what the other girls said.

Let's be kind and encourage one another. It might give someone courage to do the same.

An Extra Thought for the Extra Mile

God is our ultimate encourager. He is our cheerleader. In Zephaniah 3:17 it says, "The LORD your God is in your midst, a mighty one who will save; he will rejoice over you with gladness; he will quiet you by his love; he will exult over you with loud singing."

He rejoices over you. He celebrates with you. He quiets you with His love. He wants you to succeed. He wants you to be filled with His joy. He's in your corner. He will walk the extra mile with you.

In the moments when I struggle to be kind to others, God brings verses to mind that remind me what He has done for me and how much He loves me and the people I'm struggling to love. For example, John 3:16 says He loves us so much that He sent His Son so that I could have eternal life with Him. And

Romans 8:38-39 says absolutely nothing can separate me from the love of God. These are truths I'm learning to stand on.

I love that God always has my back. He doesn't say, "Be kind and good luck," and then leave me to figure it out. No, He gives me courage and the ability to be kind when everything in me doesn't want to be kind. I'm incredibly thankful for this.

Think back to the story of Cinderella. It was kindness that caught the prince's attention. It wasn't Cinderella's beauty, status (or lack thereof), or her abilities. Her kindness grabbed the prince's heart. When the prince first meets Cinderella, she had just run away from her house to get a break from the cruelty of her stepmother and stepsisters. She hopped on her horse and rode as fast as she could, putting space between herself and those mean women.

In a heart-stopping moment she comes face-to-face with a buck, and they stare at each other for a moment. Ella has compassion for the buck and tells him to run so he isn't killed by the hunting party searching for him. The buck rushes off, but Ella's horse follows at an extremely fast pace. The prince sees this and comes to rescue her.

What follows is a beautiful visual of how being kind to someone can alter our joy. Kindness permeates the scene. Ella is kind to the buck and the prince. She is even kind to her stepmother as she talks about her. The prince is kind in return. And this interaction completely changes Ella's posture. She entered the woods feeling the lowest she's ever felt with incredible tears streaming down her face, and she leaves the woods with a smile on her face and a renewed strength to keep on going.

Kindness changes everything. Ella was able to be kind under horrible circumstances. How often am I short with my kids after having a horrible interaction with someone? I'm totally guilty of this. If it's been a bad day, I'm not the best mom. I know Cinderella is a fictional character, but I wish sometimes I was more like her. She was always kind, and her behavior didn't change based on how she was treated. If I was in her shoes, I most likely would have given the stepmother a piece of my mind. How dare she treat me that way? But Cinderella didn't speak with anger. She didn't retaliate with hatred. She spoke with kindness.

Sometimes it is incredibly difficult to be kind. There's an old mantra that says, "If you don't have anything nice to say, don't say anything at all." If we can't find something nice to say in a situation, then we shouldn't say anything. If we can't be empathetic with someone, then we need to invite God to minister to us, search our hearts, and help us discover the emotions blocking us from showing God's mercy and love.

What about you? Is kindness in your nature as it was in Cinderella's? Or do you have to work at it as I do? Is there someone who seems to cause your joy to leak out of your cup? Maybe it's the same person every day. Maybe it's a certain situation that consumes your mind with retaliation such as when someone cuts you off on the freeway. Whatever it is for you, I challenge you today to have courage and be kind. And you'll notice your cup begin to overflow.

CHAPTER ELEVEN

Ship in a Lock

Have you ever noticed when a contestant is eliminated on a reality competition show, they usually say, "I'm grateful for the opportunity"? Sometimes I can't tell if they really mean it or if it's just the thing to say in the situation. But I love this saying. Being grateful for the opportunity is what gratitude is all about. It's not only about being grateful in the good times when we win. It's also about being grateful in the hard times when we lose.

Having an "attitude of gratitude" can be difficult. Even though I'm a glass-half-full kind of person, I struggle to be grateful. When my kids are fighting, when I'm having a hot flash for the hundredth time that day, when I look at the ten loads of laundry in need of folding, when I'm tired of being tired, it's hard to be grateful. It's more natural to dwell on the things going wrong or the things that need to change than to be grateful in the current moment.

So, why does it matter if we are grateful or not? It matters because gratitude will greatly impact our joy. It's much like a lock system on a canal. A lock system is designed like an elevator for ships. The canal is too steep for the ship to climb, so the ship moves into a lock, the gate closes behind it, and the lock fills with water. This raises the ship to the next level much like an elevator raises us from one floor to the next.

Joy and gratitude work in a similar fashion. Joy is the ship that needs to rise. Gratitude is the water that will make it rise. As gratitude floods our lives like water floods a lock, our joy rises much like the ship.

The reverse is also true. As gratitude dissipates or recedes, joy will disappear along with it.

David knew this connection between joy and gratitude intimately. He wrote many of the songs we find in the book of Psalms. Many of them find David in a difficult situation. He's either in battle or running from an enemy (most often King Saul). Yet, almost every song has an element of thanksgiving or praise to God. Psalm 7 is an example of this.

We don't know the specific situation David is writing about. He clearly is falsely charged with something. It might have been in response to the curse placed on him by Shimei (2 Samuel 16). Or it might have been in response to one of the many occasions where Saul pursued David to kill him.

Either way, David finds himself wrongfully accused and persecuted. His response is thanksgiving. Verse 1 says, "O LORD my God, in you do I take refuge; save me from all my pursuers and deliver me." Verse 17, the last verse, says, "I will give to the LORD the thanks due to his righteousness, and I will sing praise to the name of the LORD, the Most High."

I could give more examples because David wrote over seventy of the hundred and fifty chapters. No matter what situation he found himself in, David responded with thanksgiving and praise. Responding this way allowed him to rejoice and be grateful. Being grateful filled his cup with joy and gave him a reason to rejoice (even though he had no earthly reason to) and the strength and resolve to continue to be grateful.

I've been fortunate to have many women in my life model gratitude for me. My aunt was one of them. She began her cancer battle when I was in junior high school. In my early twenties, I had the opportunity to work with her and we became close. Our talks were full of wisdom, and I learned so much from her during that time. I treasured those moments.

What my aunt taught me most was gratitude. I know she had her moments of grumbling and complaining because she told me she did, but she always ended our conversations with a posture of gratitude. She would speak with a resolve that she was thankful for her life and her family. I miss those talks with her. It's been ten years since her passing, and I long to talk with her again. I am incredibly grateful for her role in my life and the life lessons she taught me.

My aunt was not the first in my family to battle cancer nor the last. My grandmother, my mom, my cousin, and my mother-in-law have all instilled in me a heart of thankfulness as they lived life through diagnosis and treatment.

For my grandmother it was thirty years of back and forth, wondering when the cancer would return. Four different times she battled. I remember when I was in fifth grade, she went to Hawaii with my grandpa and my parents. She was in remission and planned to make the most of it, grateful for every day she was given. She knew the cancer would return. It already had twice. And it did. I was in ninth grade when she died.

Through watching these amazing women, I have learned joy is found when we are grateful. Gratitude isn't forgetting about heartache and hard times or being happy all the time. Gratitude isn't only for times when everything is going well. In fact, gratitude is more necessary when things are messy and hard. Being thankful makes the hard things doable. It puts a spin on the moment. It changes the outlook. The results may not change, but the way we see things will.

I can think of so many dear friends who have gone through cancer, miscarriages, divorce, sick kiddos, or kiddos needing extra love and attention. So much heartache. So much difficulty. I can think of so many people who, by the world's standards, should be angry and bitter that so much has been taken from them.

Instead, they realize every gift is from heaven (James 1:17), and they are grateful for what they have, grateful for the time they were able to spend with loved ones now gone, and grateful for the breath in their lungs, even if their body is failing. As a result, these friends are filled with joy despite some really hard circumstances.

Don't Tell Me What to Do

If you're like me, you strongly dislike being told what to do. I'm sure I was a difficult child because I always had my own way of doing things. My daughter is much like this now. She wants to do things her way in her own timing, which rarely aligns with mine.

However, I've learned when God tells us to do something, it's for our benefit. And gratitude is encouraged and even commanded in the Bible. Colossians 3:15-17 is one of my favorite passages. It says to be thankful three different times in these three verses.

> And let the peace of Christ rule in your hearts, to which indeed you were called in one body. And be thankful. Let the word of Christ dwell in you richly, teaching and admonishing one another in all wisdom, singing psalms and hymns and spiritual songs, with thankfulness in your hearts to God. And whatever you do, in word or

deed, do everything in the name of the Lord Jesus, giving thanks to God the Father through him.

Did you catch all three? Be thankful, with thankfulness in your hearts, giving thanks to God. Just before this Paul was giving the church some encouragement on what it looks like to be a believer in Jesus. He said we have a new self now and that our old desires need to go. He says we must love and forgive and be kind. Our old selves were selfish and entitled and greedy. Our new selves in Christ, however, are free from slavery to sin. And for that we are thankful.

Psalm 100:4 says, "Enter his gates with thanksgiving, and his courts with praise! Give thanks to him; bless his name!" There are so many other verses in Scripture telling us to give thanks to God. Here are a few.

Give thanks to God for...

- ...His salvation (Isaiah 12).
- ...Our inheritance of a kingdom that cannot be shaken (Hebrews 12:28-29).
- ...His wonderful deeds (Psalm 107:8-9).
- ...His love, which endures forever (1 Chronicles 16:34).
- ...His righteousness (Psalm 7:17).
- ...Being our strength and shield (Psalm 28:7).
- ...His goodness; His steadfast love; and His faithfulness to all generations (Psalm 100:5).
- ...Being the great King above all gods (Psalm 95:2-3).
- ...His grace through Jesus Christ (1 Corinthians 1:4-5).

Paul teaches us in Philippians 4 and 1 Thessalonians 5 that we are to give thanks to God in every situation, in all circumstances, because that's His will for us. We don't have to be grateful *for* every circumstance. There are situations God does not desire for His children, and we don't have to be grateful for those. However, we can learn to give thanks to God *in* those circumstances because He is there with us and will faithfully provide all we need for life and godliness (2 Peter 1:3). And when we give thanks *in* all situations, His peace will overwhelm us.

Yet we still struggle against the impulse to complain and grumble when we are faced with life. That's just it—when things don't go *our* way, we complain. It is ingrained in our nature to desire things that make us feel good or look successful or help us to achieve. We will naturally desire for ourselves every time, which makes complaining easy and second nature while gratitude remains difficult and aloof.

So, we know gratitude is commanded, and we know it will increase our joy. But how does it play out in our everyday life? What does it look like? How do we form an "attitude of gratitude" when complaining and grumbling is our natural reaction to everyday life?

Start a Gratitude Journal

Keeping a gratitude journal is not a new idea. So many others suggest the same thing. Why? Because it works. I remember back when my children were young (infant and toddler age), I was so tired and overwhelmed and struggling a lot. My Bible study group challenged me to start a gratitude journal. I didn't really want to. I'm not the journaling type, but they dared me to do it. I like challenges, and I figured it couldn't hurt.

I accepted the challenge and committed to it for thirty days. I was shocked how much it helped. I did it publicly for accountability. I knew if I didn't post it where my group could see it, I wouldn't really do it. I posted three things every day on Facebook. Well, almost every day. I did miss a few. But doing this daily really helped put my life in perspective. I wasn't allowed to duplicate any I had done before.

The first few days I was able to come up with things to write down rather quickly. But as time progressed, I really had to think about it and contemplate how God had blessed me and what I was thankful for. It forced me to be purposeful instead of flippant with my gratitude. The more I did it, the more I focused on what I was grateful for rather than the chaos happening around me.

I discovered that when joy seems aloof, all I have to do is start thinking about all the good in my life. Being grateful for life, for family, for rain and sunshine, for every little detail of my day-to-day existence changed my perspective, and I felt joy start to return. Gratitude brings peace and contentment and joy that fills my soul.

I am going to give you the same challenge. If you're struggling with joy and gratitude, start a journal. Write three things or people or circumstances you are grateful for on a list each day. Publicly or privately, it doesn't matter. Just do it. You won't regret it!

Choose Gratitude Instead

Gratefulness requires us to dig deeper than the flesh and its desires. The flesh wants to serve itself and complain about everything. It wants to hold tightly to grudges, and it wants to win every time. If we are to combat our instincts, we must walk in step with the Spirit. That's where our power comes from. The fruit of the Spirit will replace our fleshly desires when we walk in step with Him. Paul writes the following:

> But I say, walk by the Spirit, and you will not gratify the desires of the flesh. For the desires of the flesh are against the Spirit, and the desires of the Spirit

are against the flesh, for these are opposed to each other, to keep you from doing the things you want to do. But if you are led by the Spirit, you are not under the law…But the fruit of the Spirit is love, joy, peace, patience, kindness, goodness, faithfulness, gentleness, self-control; against such things there is no law. And those who belong to Christ Jesus have crucified the flesh with its passions and desires. If we live by the Spirit, let us also keep in step with the Spirit.

—Galatians 5:16-18, 22-25

When we keep in step with the Spirit through constant communication (both prayer and reading Scripture), we can choose gratitude instead.

Choose Gratitude Instead of Frustration

We recently took a road trip to Montana. All six of us piled into the minivan and drove over thirteen hundred miles in two days. After so many hours in the car together, my frustration with my children was growing. So, in an effort to stay in step with the Spirit, I prayed for each one of my kiddos. I thanked God for what He was doing in each of their lives and for allowing me to be their mother. I thanked Him for rescuing each one of my children. And I continued my prayer of thanksgiving until the frustration dissipated. Choosing gratitude saved that road trip!

Choose Gratitude Instead of Bitterness

My dear friend watched her mom suffer through cancer, and then two years later she was diagnosed herself. Another friend of mine lost her brother to cancer. Then her little boy died of heart problems. Then her brother-in-law died a sudden death.

The world would not have thought twice if either of my friends blamed God for what happened. Life was not fair.

Yet both of my friends denied bitterness the chance to take root. Instead of blaming God, they recognized His presence in each situation and thanked Him for His comfort and peace through the darkest days in their lives. They chose gratitude instead of bitterness and walked in step with the Spirit through deep sorrow and grief.

Choose Gratitude Instead of Grumbling and Complaining

Most people don't care for rain. It is a huge inconvenience. Here in Los Angeles it makes the horrendous traffic absolutely miserable. Rainy days are gloomy and cold. The storm can cast a shadow on the day and our moods. Rain can cause us to have an "Eeyore complex" where everything is ho-hum and only so-so. Things aren't necessarily bad, but they aren't great either.

I get it, especially when the storm lasts for an extended period of time and you long to see the sun. But there is beauty in the rain too. The rain purifies the air, which is important living in Los Angeles. The skies turn from light brown to a gorgeous bright blue after the rain. It washes away the dirt on the cars and roads. Even the smell of the air changes with the rain.

And while it purifies the air, it can purify our souls as well. I love the rain because it reminds me that God washes me and purifies me every day. I feel like I can breathe a little deeper and let out a bigger sigh after a storm. It's like a fresh start or a new beginning.

This is why I love to dance in the rain. I know the beauty that is coming. Why do we wait for the storm to pass before we start rejoicing? Being thankful during the storm allows us to see the beauty *in* the storm, not just after. Having a posture of gratitude can make your worst day feel like one of the best.

And staying in step with the Spirit allows gratitude, not grumbling, to become second nature. This results in an outpouring of the fruit of the Spirit, including joy!

Have an Eternal Perspective

I am grateful God has promised to never leave me or forsake me. I am grateful He sees the big picture. I am grateful I know the ending to the story. Jesus wins, and I end up in heaven with Him where there is no more sorrow and no more pain.

When I keep this eternal perspective, gratitude comes naturally, and joy fills my soul. We struggle because it is so easy to lose this perspective. It's so easy to focus on the things we see. We don't see the big picture. We don't see the end. We see the here and now where it's bleak and difficult.

Colossians 3:2 says, "Set your minds on things that are above, not on things that are on earth." Paul was saying we need to have an eternal perspective now that we believe in Jesus Christ. We are to flee the desires of this world, including the desires to grumble and complain and become frustrated with our current circumstances. Keep focused instead on God and what He has done for us.

There's a song we sang often in our chapels in college. It says, "I get joy when I think about what He's done for me."[27] I love that song because it is so simple, yet it holds so much truth. When I think on the surface level about what I have and what God has done, it makes me happy and smile. But if I allow those thoughts to go deeper, true gratitude for what God has done for me gives me joy. Even on the worst of days when everything that could go wrong has and it feels like there is nothing currently happening that I can be grateful for, I can think about all He has done for me, and joy overflows. It comes because gratitude gives us contentment. Being content brings joy.

Choosing gratitude can change every single circumstance. It may not change the details, but it will alter our perspective. It will change how we view our circumstances. And it will certainly impact the amount of joy we have while enduring the situation. It's up to us to tap into the new and eternal perspective afforded us in Christ. Let's be like ships in a lock and watch our joy rise as we fill up with gratitude.

CHAPTER TWELVE

If You Love Me

There's one more thing we can add to our cups to ensure joy will overflow every day. That one thing is obedience. Now, I know the word obedience is loaded with all sorts of emotions. Some of you may have no issues with obedience and may even enjoy it. But there are some of you whose hairs bristle when you read this word.

Obedience can leave a bad taste in our mouths. We don't like it when other people tell us what to do. We don't like having to obey anyone. Society tells us we are our own person and shouldn't let anyone push us around. We shouldn't have to do anything we don't want to do. We're independent. Obedience is "uncool."

I remember all the cool kids at school were the ones who rebelled. They were the ones who broke the rules. And if someone followed the rules, they got teased. Names like "teacher's pet" or "goody-two-shoes" come to mind.

It seems obedience has become unnecessary. Laws have become suggestions. Of course, not the big ones like murder, but the little ones like speed limits have become subjective. The sign says, "65 mph," yet how many of us actually go sixty-five miles per hour? I know a lot of California drivers interpret sixty-five as seventy or seventy-five. Obeying this law seems unnecessary.

Another example is stop signs. I see multiple cars every single day on the walk to and from school that don't even stop at stop signs. Most of them at least slow down, but they never fully stop. Obeying this law seems unnecessary too.

Unfortunately, this sour view of obedience can taint our relationship with God. When we see man's laws as unnecessary, we begin to see God's laws as unnecessary too. For example, God says, "Honor your father and your mother" (Exodus 20:12), yet we only do it if we think they deserve it. Or what about pre-marital sex? It's completely acceptable by the culture we live in, and many believers justify it and say that waiting to have sex until marriage is old-fashioned and even oppressive. We brush disobedience off or excuse it away.

This attitude will impact our relationship with God. Just like when we disobeyed our parents when we were teenagers, creating tension in the relationship, there is tension with God when we disobey because He is holy and we are not.

God is our source of joy, and obedience to Him is necessary if we want a joy-filled soul. Joy and obedience are connected.

Obedience Produces Joy

You've heard the term "fight or flight." Those close to me would probably say "fight" unanimously if you were to ask them which one I am. I'm naturally more of a fighter. I want justice, whether for myself or someone else. My gut always tells me to fight for what's right. And I hold to my guns.

There are a handful of times however that I have instinctively chosen flight as my defense mechanism. Though circumstances were different, I very much had the same prayer Jenny had in *Forrest Gump*. "Lord, make me a bird so I can fly far, far away."[28] But in each of those moments, I felt a deep conviction that I needed to stay and process the situation. Sometimes it was the Holy Spirit leading me to a verse such as "Be still, and know that I am God," (Psalm 46:10) or "The LORD will fight for you, and you have only to be silent," (Exodus 14:14) or "Be strong and courageous. Do not be frightened, and do not be dismayed, for the LORD your God is with you wherever you go" (Joshua 1:9).

Other times it has been my husband or a good friend speaking truth into me and helping me see how running away is really the selfish option. In each of those moments, I was faced with a decision to either obey what the Lord wanted me to do or run away as fast and as far as I could.

Have you ever been in a situation where you wanted to run, and the Lord was telling you to stay? Moses certainly was. And he ran. By God's grace God used that time to equip him. Some people say it was all in God's plan for Moses to run. I think God's plan was to save the Israelites either way. He was either going to use Moses while he was in Pharaoh's house or after he had lived in the desert for forty years. God's big picture will come to play out, but our choices do impact how that happens.

There are many other stories of people faced with tough decisions of whether to obey God or not. Peter and James were thrown into prison for obeying God, and their joy grew as they continued obeying Him. Noah probably wanted to flee when he was the subject of everyone's jokes. Yet he obeyed and built the ark, and his joy overflowed (eventually).

King Hezekiah became king in a time when Israel was not following God. They worshipped idols and held to pagan beliefs.

It's all recorded in 2 Chronicles 30. King Hezekiah sought the Lord and desired to obey. He learned of certain rituals and other things that the Israelites were supposed to do but hadn't for a long time. In turn he directed the nation to turn from all idols and worship God. They did it, and there was great joy in Jerusalem, which had been absent since the time of King Solomon. Their obedience to God caused them great joy!

As I started my kids out in school, we had the opportunity to send them to a Christian school at a discounted rate. We jumped at the chance. As my kids continued their schooling, I began to see friends who homeschooled their kids, and I was liking what I saw. This desire grew as we became more and more dissatisfied with the Christian school administration. I began to research all my homeschooling options and talked with all my friends who did it. And honestly, I was ready to jump in.

But then I felt the Lord say, "I have something different in store for you." Of course, I didn't hear Him say this out loud. It was something He impressed upon my heart and mind as I prayed over our kids' schooling options. He began to open my heart to the public school system. At first I said, "No way." But I knew for certain He was saying, "That's where I want you." I didn't really want to do it.

At the time, we were looking for a new home. I asked God to prove Himself and His plan so I would have no doubt He was leading us to public school. I don't know if I already knew and was scared or if I merely wanted to know for sure, but I pulled a Gideon and put out a "fleece" (Judges 6). I said to God, "If you get us a home in this specific area (the zone for two specific elementary schools where our church hosted Good News Clubs), then I'll send them to public school. But if we get a home anywhere else, I'm homeschooling."

We looked at so many homes and put offers down on several. Not one of those homes were in the specific area I mentioned. There were simply no homes for sale in that little area. Each time we turned in another offer to buy a home, I was convinced God was saying to homeschool. But every single offer fell through.

Then out of nowhere God dropped a house in our laps. Ours was the only offer. It fell within our price range, and it was perfect for our family. And guess what? It was literally five houses away from the corner of one of the two schools. Our kids were enrolled at the public school only a few months later.

There are still days the lure of homeschooling draws me in. And maybe someday it will be what we do for our family. But for now, God has us in public school. Some of you may be thinking this is no big deal. I don't know how the schools are in your area, but our city is not known for its stellar education system. The district is making strides to improve, but it's still a long way from being the best in the county, let alone the state or nation.

The choice to send our kids to the school they now attend was not because of its test scores. It was because that is where we believe God asked us to send our kids, and we wanted to obey Him. We trusted Him and the bigger picture only He could see.

There are times I don't like that God has us in public education. I don't always like the school or the issues there, but I have come to love the people, not because they are good people (though most of them are) but because Jesus loves the people. I've come to see how a little light can shine brightly. I've seen how my children's faith has been a light to their friends and teachers. I've seen how my light has encouraged other moms and their families. God is using our family to be salt and light in our little corner, and that brings joy overflowing in abundance.

The key to our joy is not whether we are in public school or private school or homeschooling. The key to our joy is that we have been obedient to God and His leading of our family.

THE JOY FILLED SOUL

What is God asking you to do? Does it scare you? Is it uncomfortable or unknown? We often hear that we need to "step out of our comfort zone." I like to say that we need to "stretch" our comfort zone instead. Because once you've done it, it most likely will be part of your comfort zone now.

Where is God asking you to stretch and grow? Do it. Because there is no greater joy than the joy found in obedience and doing what God has asked of you. And the joy is a little sweeter when it's a result of doing something that was hard, knowing you did it because God was asking you to do it.

Jesus modeled this for us. Hebrews 12:2 says, "…who for the joy that was set before him endured the cross…" and Philippians 2:8 tells us, "…he humbled himself by becoming obedient to the point of death, even death on a cross." Jesus didn't want to die. But he chose obedience because He loves us and His Father. He knew that obedience, though it was the hardest thing to do, would lead to joy.

As an added bonus to all of this, since I am filled with joy (because I obeyed), I now want to be obedient. I have seen that following God and surrendering my life produces joy, so I want to continue to obey.

The *Shoulds*

The *shoulds* of Christianity steal our joy. We put expectations on ourselves (and others) because we think that's what makes us a good Christian. How many of these have you heard?

1. *You should read your Bible first thing in the morning.*
2. *You should put on the armor of God every day.*
3. *You should memorize Scripture.*
4. *You should tithe ten percent.*
5. *You should go to church.*

IF YOU LOVE ME

The *shoulds* have truth behind them, but they aren't meant to bring shame or discouragement. Jesus said, "If you love me, you will keep my commandments" (John 14:15). We don't obey to *earn* His love. We obey to *show* our love.

That's where the Pharisees got it wrong. They were so caught up with doing the *shoulds* and appearing obedient that they missed the message of love, grace, and mercy. They thought the more *shoulds* they performed, the better. But God created us so we could have relationship with Him, not so He could be our dictator and make us do everything He commands.

When we love someone, we want to do what they ask. It's a privilege to obey and serve when love is what motivates us. It's not a duty or obligation. When our desire is to be with God and show Him our love, then the *shoulds* of Christianity become *wants.*

The *Wants*

Obedience is not about doing more or doing better. It's not about the *shoulds* that say, "If you don't do this, you're a bad person." It's about allowing Jesus to transform us. Romans 12:2 says that we must "be transformed by the renewal of our minds." Obedience places us in a position that is ready for transformation.

The Christian life is not a collection of "I should do this" or "I should do that" checklists. When we love Jesus and desire the transformation He provides, worship is the outcome. And in worship the "I *should*" becomes "I *want.*" So, I've rewritten our *shoulds* list to say *want* instead.

1. *I want to start each day with God*

I want to start each day with God in some way because I love Him and desire to know His truth. When I begin my day with Jesus, He feeds my soul. He fills me with His truths and thoughts. Spending time reading the Bible is a great way to do this.

Other possible ways include working on memorizing His Scripture as you get ready in the morning or listening to or singing worship music, whether in the shower or on your way to work. There are many options. He is our Creator. He is our Father. He is our Friend. Starting the day with Him gives us the right perspective from the start.

Though I love in-depth Bible studies, I don't always have the time or brain bandwidth at 5:30 a.m. So, I start with a small devotional. It only takes me five minutes. But it starts my day off right. Then, later in the day or week I find the time to do the thirty-minute in-depth study that I love.

This has transformed my quiet time with God. I used to feel so much pressure to do things a certain way—the way I thought I should. But I realized the most important part is that I spend time with God each day. If I want joy, then I must spend time with the joy-giver. And I want to do it. It is not a chore. When I start my day with Jesus, I experience joy, and my demeanor and outlook for the day is so much better.

This is what works for me. Figure out what works for you because reading God's Word shouldn't be a *should.* If we love Jesus, it will be a *want.*

2. I want to put on God's Armor

I want to put on God's armor because I'm in a spiritual battle, and I can't win alone. As a kid growing up in the church, I used to think that if I didn't put on the armor, it was no big deal. Then, as an adult I quickly realized how essential the armor is. But I was still very haphazard about when I put it on, and I still didn't really take it seriously. It was as if I thought, I know

I should put on the armor, but I really don't want to. I believe in Jesus, so I'm good.

And though it is true that Jesus covers us and protects us, it is still essential we put on the armor, that we study it and know what it means and how each piece helps us in a different way. Even Jesus went into the desert at the start of His ministry with the sword—God's Word (Luke 4).

You do not need to add extra time to your morning routine to put on the armor of God. My favorite time to put on the armor is while I get ready in the morning. I memorized Ephesians 6:14-17 and so I go through each piece while I'm in the shower or drying my hair or putting on my makeup. I put on the armor while I put on my clothes.

You've heard the phrase, "I never leave home without it." Some would say that's in reference to our cell phones or our wallets. Some women never leave home without applying makeup. Let's be women who never leave home without putting on our armor, not because we must but because we want to be ready for the battle ahead of us.

3. I want to memorize Scripture

I want to memorize Scripture because it fortifies my foundation. I might have heard an audible groan on this one. Say it with me: "I want to memorize Scripture." Ladies, there are so many reasons behind this want. Jesus resisted temptation by quoting Scripture. It works the same for us. One of the first verses I learned as a kid was Psalm 119:11. "I have stored up your word in my heart, that I might not sin against you." Verse 9 says we can remain pure when we guard our hearts with Scripture.

The Bible says we "destroy arguments and every lofty opinion raised against the knowledge of God, and take every thought captive to obey Christ" (2 Corinthians 10:5). Every day I say this verse to myself so I can root out the negative or pride-filled self-talk and replace it with God's words. But it's much easier to destroy arguments and take the sinful thoughts captive when I know God's Word by memory.

We just talked about putting on the armor of God. If I didn't have the armor memorized, it wouldn't be as easy to put it on. The same goes for the fruit of the Spirit. If we want to grow the fruit, then knowing them by heart is helpful.

Philippians 4:8 says to think about true, honorable, just, pure, lovely, commendable, and excellent things. The easiest way to do this is to memorize Scripture.

We talked about being an encourager for our friends and loved ones in chapter ten. Our encouragement has awesome weight and truth when it is grounded in Scripture. So do our prayers.

Learning Scripture is so important. And once you've seen the value of having it stored in your heart, you will want to do it.

4. I want to give money back to God

I want to give money back to God because it's all His anyway. There are a lot of Scriptures on this topic. And if you've never done a study on this topic, please do so. The Bible has a lot to say about where our money comes from and what we can do with it.

My favorite is found in Matthew 6. When I finally understood what these verses meant, my giving transferred from being a *should* to a *want*.

> Do not lay up for yourselves treasures on earth, where moth and rust destroy and where thieves break in and steal, but lay up for yourselves treasures in heaven, where neither moth nor rust destroys and where thieves

do not break in and steal. For where your treasure is, there your heart will be also.

—Matthew 6:19-21

Did you catch it? It says, ". . . where your treasure is, there your heart will be also." My treasure is what I'm storing in heaven. So, my treasure is not technically my money. But what I do with my money and where I spend my money impacts what treasures I'm storing in heaven.

And where my treasure is, there my heart will be. It doesn't say, "Where my heart is, there my treasure will be." If I want my heart to be fixed on things God cares about, then I need my treasure to be fixed on things God cares about. Our hearts follow our financial investment. What are you investing in? When you are able to see that your investments are for God's glory, the *should* becomes a *want*.

5. I want to go to church

I want to go to church because corporate worship fosters community. There are a lot of things wrong with the church. That's why many people don't want to be part of one. But there are many beautiful things about the church as well.

The church is made up of believers in Jesus. These are people that have been saved by grace but are still sinners. Church isn't meant to be perfect. But the church can be a great source of joy. Worshipping God with other believers is such a beautiful experience. We are all part of the body of Christ (1 Corinthians 12). We each need to do our part for the body to succeed.

The Bible says we should not neglect to meet together (Hebrews 10:25). That's where the *should* comes from. But loving Jesus and loving His people changes that *should* to a *want* for me, and I pray it does the same for you as well.

I Don't Want To

If you love God and don't want to do the things above, I get it. I've been there. But I want to challenge you today to figure out why you don't want to start each day with God or go to church or anything else on the list. Ask yourself those questions. Let God search your heart. David asks God to do this in Psalm 139:23-24.

> Search me, O God, and know my heart! Try me and know my thoughts! And see if there be any grievous way in me, and lead me in the way everlasting!

I'm not saying that if you don't want to do these things, then you aren't a true believer. But I am saying that if you don't want to do these things, then there is something getting in your way of fully surrendering and receiving abundant joy. Maybe it's one of the things we discussed in prior chapters. Maybe it's something we haven't addressed at all. But I challenge you to figure it out. Pray about it. Ask God to search your heart like David's.

I know some of you have been hurt by people in the church. And I am so sorry for that. I've hurt people, and people have hurt me. It's harder when the hurt comes from someone in leadership, but we must remember they are susceptible to the devil and his schemes just like any of us, maybe even more so because of the damage they can cause from the top.

Whatever your reason may be for not returning to church, please pray about it. What is keeping you from wanting to be at church? Identify it and then work through it. Maybe forgiveness needs to play a role. Maybe pride needs to get out of the way. Maybe surrendering your guilt or shame needs to take place. Whatever it is, Jesus longs to have you in church with other believers, worshipping Him and making an impact toward His kingdom. And the church will be much better off with you in it, not out of it.

Sometimes we find ourselves in a dry period as David did. But he spoke with God about it. He still spent time with God each day. If you find yourself struggling with your *want*, cry out to God and tell Him. Communicate with Him. Don't shut down and push Him away because you don't feel Him. Lean in closer. Dig in deeper. He promises He will never leave us nor forsake us. We must trust Him. He always keeps His promises.

Just like a smile can change our demeanor, changing the word *should* to *want* can make a big impact in our lives. When the *shoulds* become *wants*, they stop being an obligation and start being a relationship. Jesus didn't die because He felt obligated to us. He died because He wanted to have a relationship with us. And if you love Him, you will do what He commands. We obey to show Him our love, and that obedience fills our soul with joy.

CHAPTER THIRTEEN
Mended with Purpose

There is a Japanese method of repairing broken pottery called Kintsugi. When pottery is broken, it is mended with a lacquer mixed with powdered gold, silver, or platinum. This process makes the pottery stronger and more valuable than it was before.

If we allow Jesus to mend the holes in our cups, He will make us stronger and more valuable too. We now have a joy that overflows and a testimony to share with others, rich in wisdom from our experiences of transformation by the Holy Spirit.

Remember, Jesus came to this earth to die for us so we could be reunited with our Creator, our Father. He put aside His divine nature to be just like us. He experienced life just like us. He knew we would have times when the joy in our cups would leak because of situations, circumstances, people, and pride. So, He taught the disciples (and us) everything we need to have joy to combat whatever life throws at us.

It is possible to have joy all the time. You will have sorrow. You will have trouble. Jesus said to His disciples, "In the world you will have tribulation. But take heart; I have overcome the world" (John 16:33). Don't let the worry of this world, the naysayers of this life, the shame people try to place on you decide who you are and how you'll live your life.

First, recognize what is causing the joy to leak. Then, read God's Word and become intimate with Him through prayer. Next, put into practice the steps we discussed in this book. What do you need to work on? Is it forgiveness? Is it kindness or gratitude? Is it giving worries over to God?

I know what it's like to have days, even months where it feels like you can barely keep your head above water. And some days you're confident you are going under. But practicing kindness and gratitude and studying God's Word will give you a rescue buoy to grab onto. You may still be in deep, but now your legs and arms can find relief because the life preserver is there. While you cling to that, God will mend your soul. He will fill the holes with gold while you hold onto His truths for dear life.

When I find my joy slipping away because of worry or anger or shame or anxiety or people, I push my kindness and gratitude into high gear and dig even deeper into God's Word. I've found that the more consistent I am, the less overwhelming life feels. Joy doesn't make life easy, but it gives me rest from treading water. Joy has become my permanent life preserver.

Just take one step at a time but keep taking steps. Don't stall. Don't delay. Your cup can be mended and overflowing with joy. And if we are overflowing with joy, it's naturally going to show in our lives. So, what is your response going to be?

It's Time to Rejoice

"This is the day that the LORD has made; let us rejoice and be glad in it" (Psalm 118:24). No matter what else is going on, today is good because God made it. That doesn't mean our circumstances are good or the weather is good or our health is good. It means we believe God is real and that His Word is true. We have reason to rejoice. What Jesus did for us on the cross is our reason to rejoice! We are no longer separated from God. Instead, we get to commune with Him daily because of Jesus. We get to pray directly to Him and receive His joy and peace. That is why we rejoice. Jesus is why we have joy!

There are three ways we can rejoice. We can sing. We can serve. And we can celebrate.

Sing—Make a Joyful Noise

David sang all the time. He lifted praises to Jesus on a regular basis, probably daily.

I don't know about you, but when I want to rejoice, I want to burst into song. I turn music on and let it fill my house or car. If I'm in the mood, I'll even sing at the top of my lungs as loud as I can. Sometimes I have a dance party with my kids when we want to rejoice.

When I want to rejoice and dwell in the joy of the Lord but I'm not really feeling joyful, I'll turn music on anyway. I let it fill the house, and then I start to sing even though I don't want to. Almost every single time the more I sing, the more my mood changes. Before too long I'm truly rejoicing and praising Jesus.

Sing praises to the Lord, for he has done gloriously; let this be made known in all the earth. Shout, and sing for joy, O inhabitant of Zion, for great in your midst is the Holy One of Israel.

—Isaiah 12:5-6

This is only one of many Scriptures telling us to sing and shout for joy. In Exodus 15 Moses sings to the Lord for rescuing the people of Israel from the hand of Pharaoh. Deborah and Barak "make melody to the Lord" in Judges 5:3 after the Israelites destroyed Jabin, king of Canaan. David, of course, sings to the Lord throughout his life and records many of his songs in the book of Psalms. Zephaniah foretells of the singing that will happen when Jerusalem is restored and Israel is made whole again (Zephaniah 3:14). Paul instructs believers to be "filled with the Spirit" and to make "melody to the Lord with your heart" (Ephesians 5:18-19).

My favorite hymn is "His Eye is On the Sparrow." Every time I sing it or hear it, a peace comes over me, and my soul overflows with joy. God is watching over each one of us, and His Word says He loves us and cares for us even more than the sparrow, whom He cares for very much. Not one dies without Him knowing. How much more does God care for us?

Civilla Martin visited her dear friend Mrs. Doolittle in the spring of 1905. Mrs. Doolittle was bedridden, and her husband was in a wheelchair, yet they were filled with a contagious joy. Mrs. Martin commented on Mrs. Doolittle's "bright hopefulness" and asked her about it. Mrs. Doolittle responded, "His eye is on the sparrow, and I know He watches me." Mrs. Martin said it was the "beauty of [Mrs. Doolittle's] simple expression of boundless faith [that] gripped the hearts and fired the imagination of Dr. Martin and me."[29] She wrote a poem that same day and then sent it to Charles Gabriel, a composer, and it quickly became a favorite hymn of many.

The chorus starts with the line "I sing because I'm happy." I am taking some liberties here, but I think Mrs. Martin would have said, "I sing because my soul is filled with joy," if it had fit into her poem.

Mrs. Doolittle was filled with Jesus. She had peace about life even though she was bedridden for over twenty years. She wasn't grumpy, angry, discontent, or bitter. She allowed the joy of the Lord to fill her life. That confidence and outlook on life came from her knowledge and belief of the Scriptures. She knew God loved her and cared for her. She trusted His Word to be true. And that trust made her joy overflow.

And now my joy overflows when I sing the song inspired by her life. "I sing because I'm happy, I sing because I'm free, His eye is on the sparrow, and I know He watches me."[30]

I sing because I'm filled with joy.

I sing because I'm free. Jesus said in John 8:34 that we are slaves to sin, but He has set us free. As believers in Jesus we are free from the bondage of sin. Paul says, "Now the Lord is the Spirit, and where the Spirit of the Lord is, there is freedom" (2 Corinthians 3:17). That should cause us to sing and shout. Freedom causes us to rejoice!

If we are free, then why are we walking around with no joy as though there is a chain around our necks? Why aren't we rejoicing? Why aren't we singing and dancing as the Israelites did so often (Exodus 15:20; Psalm 149:3; Psalm 150:4)?

We have many reasons to rejoice and sing: the hope of the glory of God (Romans 5:2), our names being written in heaven (Luke 10:20), God takes care of our every need (1 Samuel 2:1), and so many more.

When was the last time you sang praises to the Lord? (And not in church when you have to sing.) When was the last time you shouted for joy because the Holy One is in your midst?

Sing to the Lord today!

Serve—In Your Joy Spot

You are overflowing with joy. What are you going to do now? As much as you may want "going to Disneyland" to be your answer, the best answer is to share your joy with others. Some say Disneyland is the "happiest place on earth," and it is a fabulous place to be. However, serving Jesus is the "most joy-filled place on earth." When we take our joy and use it to serve others, it is truly marvelous.

You can serve anywhere in any way. God wants to use you to bring joy to people's lives. But I'm going to go a step further. Although you can serve anywhere, your joy will overflow a hundred times over when you serve using the gifts God has given you.

There is a time and a place for filling in for someone in an area that does not bring you joy, that isn't what you are passionate about. But long-term service should be in the place God designed you to be. You'll know you're where God designed you to be because it will align with your gifts and passions. It will bring you joy.

Some of us are blessed to have a day job that connects our passions and talents while some of us do not. But nothing should keep us from serving in a way that utilizes the gifts and passions God has given us. There is danger if we don't serve in this way; we may develop bitterness and apathy instead of joy.

I fought this for years. I let the "duty" or "responsibilities" of a Christian dictate where I served. I served where I was needed, not where I was gifted. I tried to do it with a willing heart, but there were days I simply did not want to serve. It transitioned from a service to an obligation. When I started serving in the area that utilized my skill set, however, it unlocked a new level of joy in me. And that made me want to serve even more.

If you don't like serving Jesus in your local church, then maybe you're serving in the wrong area. Own your gifts. Own the passions and ideas God gave you and use them for His glory! That's the point. If we only use our gifts in our basement, then we're limiting joy in our lives and joy in others' lives. Sharing our talents is doing our part of being a member in the body of Christ (Romans 12).

Please serve at church in whatever area brings you joy. Don't serve simply because there is a need. Too many times I've seen people serve with children, and they hate it (and in turn the kids hate it). I appreciate their desire to help, but they know this is not where they are gifted, nor does it bring them joy.

I'm not talking about those moments when the nursery worker is sick and you step up to help. I'm talking about Sunday after Sunday serving in an area you dread. God desires to bring you joy as you use the talents He gave you. Pray to know where that is and then serve with abandon.

We are all different with diverse skill sets. When we realize those skills and live, serve, and do life with those skill sets, we are all better off. I'm not saying you shouldn't try new things, and I'm not giving you a free pass to never clean your house again because "cleaning is not in my skill set." (Though I truly wish this were the case.) I am saying that when we stop trying to be everyone else and start being the person God made us to be, everyone benefits. Once you find your "joy spot," stay there. Serve there. Give God the glory there!

Celebrate—Make a Joy List

What makes you happy? What fills your soul? Sometimes we need little things to remind us joy is just beneath the surface.

When we believe in Jesus and have the Holy Spirit residing within us, when we are abiding with Him, joy is always possible. We only need to be reminded sometimes that it's within our reach.

I was making centerpieces for our communion meal at church. It was springtime, so beautiful flowers were involved. I had tulips and chamomile. Until I purchased it at Trader Joe's, I didn't know what chamomile looked like. My favorite flowers have always been daisies. So, when I came across these itty-bitty flowers, I grabbed them. They would work perfectly as fillers for my tulips. Little did I know how much joy they would bring into my life.

A few days later I had the leftover flowers sitting on my windowsill. I had just had a rough night with my son. Parenting a tween is not for the faint of heart. It was ten o'clock at night. I was standing over my sink, finishing up some dishes from the day with tears streaming down my face. I couldn't figure this kid out. I didn't know how to help him. I looked up, and there in my window was the bouquet of leftover chamomile. It immediately brought a smile to my face. And as I stared at the flowers, God reminded me that joy during this desert place with my son is possible. I don't have all the answers, but as I stood there, praying for discernment and wisdom, I was reminded to smile and "smell the chamomile."

That little mason jar filled with tiny flowers seems so insignificant. But God used that small, insignificant thing to remind me that joy is just below the surface. What is it in your life that brings a smile to your face? Maybe it's music. Maybe it's a good book. Maybe it's being outside in nature. Maybe it's traveling and seeing all the amazing places God has created.

Make a list of things that bring you joy. This list is more than a mere gratitude list. I'm grateful for my house, and I'm grateful for my kids' clothes, but cleaning both of them does not bring me joy. God uses many things to bring joy into our lives. Every good and perfect gift comes from our Father in heaven (James 1:17). And those perfect gifts add to our joy. Here are a few things that are on my joy list.

His Presence

I know there are times in every one of our lives that we feel God is distant. It can be in the darkest times as we wonder where God is as the bad stuff unfolds. It can also be in the happiest of times because we don't seem to need Him as close. But the truth is God is always present, and that is a gift.

So many verses remind us that God promises He will never leave us. My favorite is found in Deuteronomy 31:6. "Be strong and courageous. Do not fear or be in dread of them, for it is the LORD your God who goes with you. He will not leave you or forsake you." The truth that He is always there, protecting me and guiding me, will bring me joy every time. It's the moment when you realize you can let out a deep sigh because God is there, and everything is going to be okay. No matter what happens, everything will be okay.

His Word

I can't begin to share how many times His Word has brought me joy. No matter what mood I'm in or what situation I'm enduring, God's Word has brought comfort, peace, and ultimately joy. One passage I can always count on is Psalm 27. Here are a few of my favorite verses.

> The LORD is my light and my salvation; whom shall I fear? The LORD is the stronghold of my life; of whom shall I be afraid?…Though an army encamp against me, my heart shall not fear; though war arise against me, yet I will be confident. One thing have I asked of

the LORD, that will I seek after: that I may dwell in the house of the LORD all the days of my life, to gaze upon the beauty of the LORD and to inquire in his temple. For he will hide me in his shelter in the day of trouble; he will conceal me under the cover of his tent; he will lift me high upon a rock...Hear, O LORD, when I cry aloud; be gracious to me and answer me! You have said, "Seek my face." My heart says to you, "Your face, LORD, do I seek." ...Teach me your way, O LORD, and lead me on a level path because of my enemies. Give me not up to the will of my adversaries; for false witnesses have risen against me, and they breathe out violence. I believe that I shall look upon the goodness of the LORD in the land of the living! Wait for the LORD; be strong, and let your heart take courage; wait for the LORD!

—Psalm 27:1, 3-5, 7-8, 11-14

My Brothers and Sisters in Christ

Laughter. Friendship. Living life together. All these things bring me so much joy. Paul calls his fellow believers in Philippi his "joy and crown" (Philippians 4:1). I would say that about my church family too.

Quality Time with My Family

I love spending quality time with my family. Whether it's a hike, a road trip, a quest to find the best donut, playing board games, cooking breakfast on the beach, or snuggling up for a movie night—being with my family fills my cup with joy.

Nature

It is difficult for me to be grumpy when I'm out in God's creation. When I'm in the mountains, hiking or sitting outside, soaking in His goodness, my cup overflows.

A little creek flows through the edge of the summer camp I grew up attending. It has trees and dense vegetation downstream. Upstream is a meadow and an old, rundown cabin. In the middle of this creek is a giant rock. I could sit on this rock for hours. In fact, I have. I've read God's Word on that rock. I've sung worship songs on that rock. I've sat and cried while listening to the bubbling brook flow past on all sides. And every single time peace and joy fill my soul. Now I don't even have to go there. I can just think of it, and a calm comes over me, and joy abounds.

Music

So often when I listen to the radio and a commercial for the radio station comes on, the people say things like, "I had a horrible day. Then I turned on your radio station, and it brightened my day. It made my day better." Why is that? It's because music brings joy.

So many songs lift my spirit. Some songs have been favorites for years. Others have been only for a season or a moment.

I'm sure you can think of at least one song that brings a smile to your face and makes you want to shout with joy.

Mended with Purpose

It's time to act. Joy is not something you sit and soak up like the sun. Joy is something you must actively seek, fight for, and grab hold of.

Be careful. Sometimes it's in the mundane things of life where we aren't going through a trial or hard time that joy can easily fall below the surface. When we don't have to fight hard for something, it can easily get pushed aside or covered. Doing dishes every day may not be puncturing my cup, but it certainly does not fill my cup either.

Be proactive with your joy-filled soul. When I do dishes or laundry, I usually listen to music or podcasts. This ensures that my joy stays at the surface and doesn't dip below during the mundane, not-so-fun parts of life. It also ensures a grateful attitude rather than a grumbling one.

Remember, joy motivated Jesus to endure the cross (Hebrews 12). Joy is what should motivate us to keep on keeping on. The hope that lies with eternity is ours to possess.

We have been mended with purpose.

Ladies today is the day the Lord has made. Embrace the joy He longs to give you. Let it overflow your cup. And share it with everyone. We can change the world when we are filled with joy. Let His truths transform you and give you peace and contentment, and may you have a joy-filled soul.

Let's Connect!

I'd love to hear about your journey to a

Joy Filled Soul

Use
#TheJoyFilledSoul

Message me on
Instagram @janinelansing or
Facebook @janine.e.lansing

Left wanting more?
Find additional resources at
JanineLansing.com

LIVE in the Spirit, LINGER with Jesus, & LOVE God's Word!

Acknowledgements

There are many people who contributed in some way to The Joy Filled Soul. I'd like to say thank you…

To The Joy Filled Soul book prayer team—words cannot express the support I felt from all of you from the very beginning. You lovingly prayed for me through this process and I am incredibly grateful. And to my launch team. You all believed in the message of this book and gave it wings. Thank you!

To Josie, Tammie, Stacey, and Dana—you are very dear friends who have always loved me, even in my ugliness, and have gently but vocally guided me towards Christ.

To Christy—you helped me find the words that expressed what was in my heart and guided me to a proper understanding of God's Word.

To Author Academy Elite Publishing—you took a chance on this girl who had a message to write but had no clue how to do it. To my amazing coaches and editors Niccie, Kary, Brenda,

Nanette, Abigail, and Veloie—you helped me find my voice and purpose. To Debbie—my cover designer, you took a vision in my head and turned it into something that makes me smile from ear to ear.

To my family, biological and spiritual—thank you for loving me through it all. Your spoken and unspoken support spoke volumes to my heart. To the ladies at WOW Bible study—you restored in me a love for God's Word. You helped develop a passion that has not ceased. Thank you!

To my children, Wesley, Tyler, Rylee, and Hannah—you are my joy spot. I love being your mom. Thank you for loving me and forgiving me and helping me see Jesus everyday.

To my amazing hubby, Timothy—you have been my cheerleader from day one. You have always encouraged me, helped me dream, and believed in this book before I even knew it was a reality. Thank you for providing a shoulder to cry on, keeping the kiddos entertained while I wrote, and pushing me to see what is possible.

To God, my Creator—You entrusted me with Your message. Thank You for loving me and teaching me who You are. Your sacrifice for me is unfathomable and I will shout it from the mountaintops as long as I'm able. You are my breath. May this book be Your message, not mine and may You be glorified!

Small Group
Discussion Guide

Dear Small Group Leader,

Thank you for being a small group leader. Thank you for stepping up and being the organizer and cheerleader of those God has placed in your life. I know it's often a thankless job, but I want you to know that I appreciate what you do every week. And thank you for taking your small group through my book. My prayer is that it will encourage you all as you meet to encourage each other.

Here are a few questions to guide you through your small group discussion. You can ask all of them or just a few of them, and the order doesn't matter. These are meant to start the conversation about the transformation Jesus is doing in the lives of your group members.

Small Group Questions:

- What is something you underlined in this chapter that you would like to share with the group?
- Did you have an "aha moment" this week? If so, will you share it with us?
- What was your main take away from this chapter?
- Were you able to identify anything causing your joy to leak?
- How did your soul mend this week?
- How did your soul fill with joy this week?
- Was there anything you didn't understand or had questions about?

May I pray for you as you embark on this journey of leading others to a joy-filled soul?

Dear God,

Thank You for this small group leader who is taking this next step to lead Your children on a quest to be filled with Your joy. I ask that You fill her with the knowledge of Your will in all spiritual wisdom and understanding, so she may walk in a manner worthy of You, fully pleasing to You. May this journey bear fruit and increase her knowledge of You as she helps other women do the same. It is Your glorious might that will strengthen her and give her courage. Please give her endurance and patience with joy as she gives thanks to You. You chose her for this and qualified her to share in the blessings You give. May the words of her mouth and the meditation of her heart be her worship to You. We love You and we ask for Your blessing over this small group. In Jesus's name, Amen!

Notes

1. G. W. Cooke, "Joy in My Heart," copyrighted 1925 (unrenewed).
2. "There's a Hole in My Bucket" in *Songs Along the Mahantongo: Pennsylvania Dutch Folk-songs,* ed. Boyer, Buffington, and Yoder (Lancaster: Pennsylvania Dutch Folklore Center, 1951).
3. Debby Kerner and Ernie Rettino, "Cares Chorus," written by Kelly Willard, recorded 1985, track 9 on *Kids' Praise! 5: Psalty's Camping Adventure...Count It All Joy!*, Maranatha! Music, Vinyl LP.
4. Merriam-Webster, s.v. "Joy," https://www.merriam-webster.com/dictionary/joy.
5. Winston Churchill, *The Wit and Wisdom of Winston Churchill,* ed. Max Morris (Chichester, West Sussex: Summersdale Publishers, 2016).

6. NAS Old Testament Hebrew Lexicon, s.v. "Nephesh," https://www.biblestudytools.com/lexicons/hebrew/nas/nephesh.html

7. Merriam-Webster, s.v. "Abide," https://www.merriam-webster.com/thesaurus/abide.

8. Merriam-Webster, s.v. "Desire," https://www.merriam-webster.com/dictionary/desire.

9. Dan Allender and Tremper Longman, *The Cry of the Soul: How Our Emotions Reveal Our Deepest Questions About God* (Colorado Springs: NavPress, 1994), 25-26.

10. Bryan White, "Someone Else's Star," co-written by Skip Ewing and Jim Weatherly, recorded 1994, track 4 on *Bryan White*, Asylum Records, CD.

11. Lauren Barlow, *Inspired by Tozer: 59 Artists, Writers and Leaders Share the Insight and Passion They've Gained from A.W. Tozer* (Ada Township: Baker Publishing Group, 2011), 121.

12. "Anxiety Disorders," National Institute of Mental Health, http://www.nimh.nih.gov/health/topics/anxiety-disorders/index.shtml.

13. NAS New Testament Greek Lexicon, s.v. "Merimnao," https://www.biblestudytools.com/lexicons/greek/nas/merimnao.html.

14. Keith Minier, "Daily Comebacks," July 19, 2017, Momentum Youth Conference, Marion, Indiana, United States.

15. NAS Old Testament Hebrew Lexicon, s.v. "Leb," https://www.biblestudytools.com/lexicons/hebrew/nas/leb.html.

16. VeggieTales, "God is Bigger," track 2 on *VeggieTunes,* released November 22, 1995, Everland Entertainment, CD.

17. *Mary Poppins*, directed by Robert Stevenson (Burbank, CA: Buena Vista Distribution, 1964), VHS.

18. Horatio Spafford, author, "It Is Well," composed by Philip Bliss, written 1873.

19. *Pete's Dragon*, directed by Don Chaffey (Burbank, CA: Buena Vista Distribution, 1977), VHS.
20. Max Lucado, *You Are Special* (Wheaton: Crossway Books, 1997).
21. *The Today Show*, episode 1080, produced by Tammy Filler, featuring Dylan Dreyer (weather anchor), aired April 22, 2019, on NBC.
22. Nathaniel Hawthorne, *The Scarlet Letter* (Boston: Ticknor and Fields, 1850).
23. Melissa Spoelstra, *Joseph – Women's Bible Study Participant Book: The Journey to Forgiveness* (Nashville: Abingdon Press, 2015).
24. *Little House on the Prairie,* episode 4, "Mr. Edward's Homecoming," directed by Michael Landon, written by Blanche Hanalis, aired October 2, 1974, on NBC.
25. *Cinderella*, directed by Kenneth Branagh (Burbank, CA: Walt Disney Studio Productions, 2015), DVD.
26. *The Lord of the Rings: The Fellowship of the Ring*, directed by Peter Jackson (Los Angeles, CA: New Line Cinema, 2001), DVD.
27. "I Get Joy", traditional gospel song, author unknown.
28. *Forrest Gump*, directed by Robert Zemeckis (Hollywood: Paramount Pictures, 1994), DVD.
29. Emilie Barnes, *Walk with Me Today, Lord* (Eugene: Harvest House Publishers, 2008), 29.
30. Civilla D. Martin, "His Eye Is on the Sparrow," composed by Charles H. Gabriel, published 1905.

CPSIA information can be obtained
at www.ICGtesting.com
Printed in the USA
BVHW031402150720
583806BV00004B/369